# MODERN LOVE

D1202597

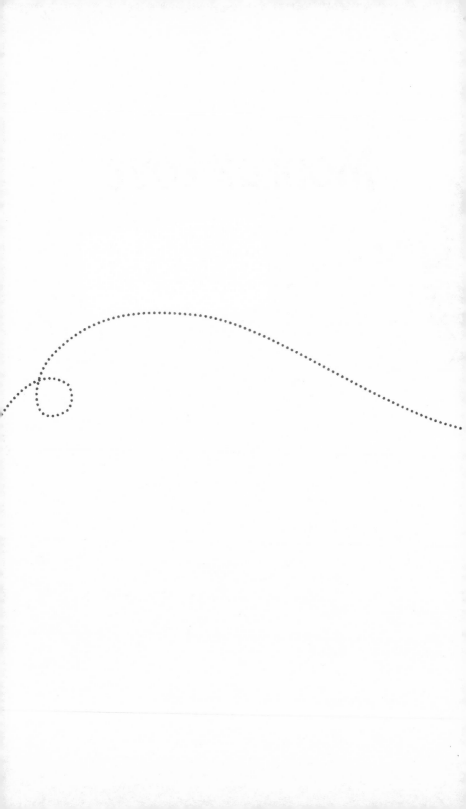

# MODERN LOVE

## A No-Nonsense Guide
## To a Life of Passion

by Sallie Foley

ILLUSTRATIONS BY JEFFREY FISHER

STERLING PUBLISHING CO., INC.

AARP Books publishes a wide range of titles on health, personal finance, lifestyle, and other subjects to enrich the lives of older Americans. For more information, go to www.aarp.org/books

AARP, established in 1958, is a nonprofit organization with more than 35 million members age 50 and older. The recommendations and opinions expressed herein are those of the author and do not necessarily reflect the views of AARP.

The AARP name and logo are registered trademarks of AARP, used under license to Sterling Publishing Co., Inc.

Library of Congress Cataloging-in-Publication Data Available

10  9  8  7  6  5  4  3  2  1

Published in paperback in 2006 by Sterling Publishing Co., Inc.
387 Park Avenue South, New York, NY  10016
© AARP 2005
Distributed in Canada by Sterling Publishing
c/o Canadian Manda Group, 165 Dufferin Street
Toronto, Ontario, Canada  M6K 3H6
Distributed in the United Kingdom by GMC Distribution Services,
Castle Place, 166 High Street, Lewes, East Sussex, England BN7 1XU
Distributed in Australia by Capricorn Link (Australia) Pty. Ltd.
P.O. Box 704, Windsor, NSW 2756, Australia

*All rights reserved*
*Manufactured in the United States of America*

Sterling ISBN-13: 978-1-4027-1738-3  Hardcover
        ISBN-10: 1-4027-1738-5
        ISBN-13: 978-1-4027-4075-6  Paperback
        ISBN-10: 1-4027-4075-1

For information about custom editions, special sales, or premium and corporate purchases, please contact the Sterling Special Sales Department at 800-805-5489 or specialsales@sterlingpub.com

For the readers of the
"Modern Love" Column
*Your questions mad this book possible.*
*And without you, there'd be no answers.*

For Steve
*Thanks for asking your question.*
*After 28 years, the answer is still yes!*

# Contents

# Introduction

THE LOVE LIVES of older Americans are as varied and vital as those of their twentysomething counterparts, yet they are complex and confusing in ways no postadolescent could grasp. As a marital and sex therapist in private practice since 1985, I've been asked to untangle the complexity and confusion of hundreds of couples' relationships and sexual dilemmas. I've heard tales from all bandwidths of the sexual-experience spectrum, from the couple married 50 years who claimed, "Not even a prison sentence lasts this long!" to the couple who had their first successful sexual experience at age 50 and demanded to know, "What took us so long?!"

In the pages that follow, you'll find advice of all kinds, and lots of it, both for people who feel caught in connubial prisons and for those so content in their tender trap they want to throw away the key. All of the questions were submitted by readers of the "Modern Love" column in *AARP The Magazine*.

Sexual security, AARP research reveals, is a vital and ongoing concern for older Americans. In 2004, following up on a study it first conducted in 1999, AARP surveyed sexual attitudes among those 45 and older. If you've read this far, the results probably won't surprise you: Most of those polled view sexual activity as important in their relationships, and they view sexual satisfaction as a key to the quality of their lives. Among the survey's more intriguing results: The number of people seeking answers to their sexual questions from health professionals, the Internet, and friends is markedly on the rise. And that's a good thing: It means that talking about sex is becoming a normal, healthy part of life.

If the term "sex therapist" conjures up leather skirts and stiletto heels, you headed down the wrong neuropathway (not that there's anything *wrong* with that...). We're mental health professionals—counselors—with specialized training in sex education and treating problems in sexual functioning. We work in mental health clinics or have psychotherapy practices of our own. A few times a year we gather at national conventions—such as that of the American Association of Sex Educators, Counselors, and Therapists (www.aasect.org)—where we hang out with one another and learn new and interesting things.

Lots of us are married.

Many have children.

All worry about things that have nothing to do with sex.

And oh yes, we're a pretty normal-looking group, too. One year our conference took place next door to a convention of garage-door salesmen. You really couldn't tell us apart on the elevators—except that one group seemed discomfited by the other.

I want to applaud my (and everyone else's) patients, because it takes real courage to seek counseling from a marital or sex therapist. Think of how it feels to discuss the intimate details of household finance with your accountant; now multiply that sensation by a factor of 20. When I first meet with a couple, I am often impressed that they care

enough about themselves and their relationship to seek
professional advice from a complete stranger about the most
private corners of their lives. At other times, I feel dejected
—dejected that a couple waited so long to seek help that it
was "all over but the shoutin'."

People turn to professionals for a panoply of reasons:
Arguments. Stress with kids. Money problems. Loneliness
or alcohol. Boredom, betrayal, divorce—and all that is just
before my lunch hour. Sometimes the problem is longstand-
ing, as it was for the couple I counseled (unsuccessfully, it
turned out) at 45; married 20 years, they had each carried
on a string of affairs since their late 20s. At other times, the
problem is newly minted; I'm thinking of the woman who
relished sex until she hit menopause, or the 55-year-old
man who started having anxiety attacks in the wake of
being downsized from his job.

Whereas counseling can redirect the course of some
lives, it seems not to sway others in the least. Still, the very
act of seeking advice is as old as humanity itself; Eve didn't
choose the best advisor, but she was open to learning.

As you'll gather from the questions and answers in
Modern Love, marital and sex therapists are nosy by nature.
We are psychologically inquisitive about life. We want to
know what makes people tick—and what sets their alarm
bells clanging.

In my own career, this curiosity had a circuitous effect:
It led me on a three-year detour through Princeton Theo-
logical Seminary and Drew University Graduate School
of Theology. (I leave it to you to draw the obvious confes-
sional parallels between minister and therapist.) I like
to think my skill at answering practical questions was

honed by all those years of contemplating the eternal ones.

Sex therapy was still far in my future, though; after com-
pleting graduate school in social work, I spent the next
eight years working with cancer patients—both children
and adults—at the University of Michigan Hospitals. Those
folks taught me the meaning of true passion for life. Spouses
would climb into hospital beds to cuddle their patient-
partners. Single people, their heads turbaned and their eyebrows eradicated by chemotherapy, swapped survival stories
—and phone numbers. If you're not dead, I learned, you
resent being treated like a corpse, and an oncologist who
waltzes a woman wearing a hospital gown and dragging an
IV pole will never be forgotten.

In 1982, a handful of those visionaries from the departments of Obstetrics and Gynecology and Social Work
opened the doors of Sexual Health Counseling Services in
Ann Arbor, Michigan. When they offered me a job as a sex
therapist, I suddenly discovered where my lifelong fascination
with the unknown and the unmentionable had been leading
me. Three years of training with experts in psychotherapy
and human sexuality were necessary before I finally reached
my goal: certification as a sex therapist by AASECT.

Along the way, people invariably asked me, "What's it
like to be a sex therapist?"

"It's just like being any other therapist," I would explain,
"except that I can say dirty words without blushing."

From the beginning, I've had an opportunity to learn
from some exceptional pioneers in the field: Elisabeth
Kübler-Ross on death and dying; William Masters and
Virginia Johnson on human sexuality; Geri Chipault and
Joann Langlie on social work practice. I've been equally for-

tunate to work with terrific colleagues in a truly interdisci-
plinary setting. The headaches, when they come, stem
mainly from my bad habit of overloading my own plate in
such a lively place.

Sex and marital therapists need balance in their lives.
Otherwise they would never stop talking about life and
start living it. That's just one of the reasons I'm so grateful
to have married a person who is patient (I'm not), good-
humored (I'm learning), and laid back (what was that term
again?). We're the parents of three kids—identical twin
daughters and a son. Being in a partnership and raising
a family together has been the best teacher of life's true
priorities: If nothing humbles like the daily grind, nothing
exalts like special moments shared with the people you love.

So there's a peek inside *my* emotional background. This
is the memory bank I draw upon as I respond to clients or
readers, reassuring them that everyone struggles to repair
or refurbish a relationship, and that everyone obsesses about
sex or love at some point—often many—in their lives.

Is your own relationship quandary or sexual question
addressed in these pages? Although it's difficult for me to
read your aura from here, I'd have to say your odds are
good. As long as you possess curiosity and desire, you've
come to the right place.

—SALLIE FOLEY

# Finding New Love

*It's not the men in my life,
it's the life in my men that counts.*
—MAE WEST

# Finding New Love

WHICH WOULD YOU CHOOSE: dating after 40 or an industrial-strength wedgie? If you chose the latter, you're not alone. Whereas a wedgie is a known discomfort, the dating game abounds with miseries unimagined: Most people would steer a million miles clear of its uncertainty, its self-consciousness, its utter absence of guidelines if they possibly could. And whereas a wedgie inflicts only temporary anguish (one hopes), dating at 40+ can sometimes seem like a sentence served in perpetuity.

Finding a new love later in life is fraught with liabilities, among them making people feel touchy about the shape of their assets. Even in this supposedly enlightened era, we're still fighting the preconception that men calculate their appeal in terms of financial success, whereas women compute theirs in terms of allure and desirability. Yet the fear of being turned down by someone you deem worthy of your emotional investment seems to defy both gender and age; it's an equal-opportunity humiliation.

If anyone above the age of 40 dared to write a real-life personal, it might read something like this:

"*Honest age here* older adult looking for love. I have baggage: My body is not what it used to be, but I do love to move it. My kids are almost grown; my elderly parents take the rest of my time. I'm either widowed and still yearning for my spouse, or divorced and still bruised from the experience.

"Whether I'm working or retired, I never seem to have enough money to cover everything, so please don't answer this ad unless you're financially solvent. I'm basically a shy person, more cautious than I used to be—more of a worrier too, come to think of it.

"On the upside, I've developed a fierce capacity to follow through on life. I've got a wicked sense of humor, and my passion—when tapped—is as bountiful as ever. I have the kind of friends that move mountains, and I've moved a few myself (both friends and mountains). Despite the mileage under my belt, the heart in my chest is young—and I'm eager to share it."

If you can relate to any aspect of that midlife manifesto, read on. Chances are you'll find some questions in these pages that are remarkably similar to your own. You may not agree with all of my answers—in fact, I hope to hear from you if you don't (see page 154). Nor do you need to be playing the field in order to find your own raw life experiences reflected here.

Finally, I've asked a few favorite writers to contribute sidebars on such hot-button issues as older lovers (page 25), online dating (page 39), and falling in lust again (page 47). Now bring those questions on!

# 1

# Back in the Game Again

**Q** I'm an attractive single older woman. I've noticed that men my age seem to be attracted to women 20 years younger. How can I overcome this?

**A** You can have two viewpoints about this. The first involves a little understanding: Naturally, men are attracted to younger women. After all, 25 years ago you were a big problem for women in their 50s. The second is an indictment: Midlife men are insecure about their virility, so they need the ego boost of snagging a younger woman; that is, men are superficial pigs. The second attitude is quite common and counterproductive. If you're angry at men for being attracted to Jennifer Lopez—for being, well... men, others will detect your edginess and interpret it as defensiveness about your age.

"If you assume, even subconsciously, that a man won't be interested in you, that may take you out of the flirtation game," explains Los Angeles sexologist Patti Britton, Ph.D., an expert for iVillage.com. "You've got to feel playful, and carrying resentment makes that difficult."

That said, there are ways to hook up with men your own age. First, consider trying online dating services, such as Match.com, Matchmaker.com, and Great-Expectations.net. They've evolved into great resources for mature people who are seeking romantic partners with particular characteristics, be it a taste for fine wine or an interest in women who know far more about romance than counterparts half their age.

Second, make an effort to stay as fit as you can. It will make you vital, optimistic. "Keeping yourself healthy, your attitude vivacious, and your heart open is a great blessing," says Barnaby Barratt, president of the American Association of Sex Educators, Counselors, and Therapists. "Beauty and sexiness come from energy."

Third, keep playing the gender card. If you ask me, too many attractive women our age settle for a gender-lite look by dressing more unisex than they once did. (Sure, you can argue that a lot of middle-aged guys aren't exactly slaving over their appearance, either, but we're talking about you here.) So don't be afraid to mix comfort with a dash of come-on.

Finally, the most attractive quality a person can have, at any age, is confidence—that aura of joyfulness and self-possession that tells the world you're enjoying a rich life. It's tough to project if you don't feel it, but give it a try. You may start to feel the sentiment you're feigning. "Attitude is everything," says Barratt. "Focus on loving and valuing yourself—this will make you immensely alluring to those around you."

**Q** The woman I've started seeing revealed to me that she's also dating another man. I'm newly divorced and haven't dated for many years, so I'm not sure how to deal with this. Is this normal? Can I expect us to go forward?

**A** What she's doing is pretty common. Getting phone messages from Moe, Larry, and Curly can make a woman feel beautiful and desired—especially if she's just out of a long relationship with the same tedious, God-rest-his-soul, guy. And, obviously, it can make her social life far more fun.

"Some multiple daters go out with several people to keep things from getting too serious too fast," explains AASECT President Barnaby Barratt. Spreading her bets can also prevent a woman from becoming too attached to a man who may not stick around (a defensive tactic she's learned through experience).

At the far end of the casual dating spectrum, notes Barratt, there are people who believe in having ongoing multiple relationships without ever settling down with just one person. This unusual practice even has a name: polyamory.

"She's done you the honor of being upfront about her situation," says Barratt. Don't take that lightly; it can be rare to find such frank honesty in dating. If you're enjoying getting to know her, don't bail just because she's filling her dance card. Barratt's advice: Steer your next conversation toward the topic of relationships, and ask about her views. Is she looking for a long-term monogamous relationship, as I'm assuming you are? If that's the case, you have two options.

The first choice is the "bring-on-the-competition" strategy, in which you keep dating her and are so darn thoughtful, charming, and enthused that she forgets all about Joe Competitor.

Don't like your odds in a one-on-one against the guy? Opt for the "you're-great-but-I-can't-handle-this" strategy. Tell her respectfully that you just can't deal with sharing her. Sound apologetic for being so old-fashioned. Important: This cannot be an ultimatum. If she hears even a trace of "It's him or me," you'll lose. A good line: "I think the world of you, but we seem to want different things right now. I'd love to hear from you in the future." Show her a self-reliant man who knows what he wants, and she may not let you go.

Finally, an obvious concern: If both of her relationships are sexual, this situation raises health issues—even if you're using protection. Many people find monogamy tricky enough without trying to juggle the emotional complexity of a sexual triangle.

**Q** My wife died two years ago, and I think I'm ready to date, just for companionship. But after many years of being with one person, I have no idea where to begin. How do you get back in the dating game again?

A Let your friends know you're prepared to start dating again, then sit back and watch the matchmakers work. And don't worry—the rules of the game didn't change all that much while you were married. Dating still uses the classic three-part plan: 1) See woman. 2) Talk to woman. 3) Call woman up, and take your shot. To calm your nerves, don't think of it as "dating." You're only looking to see where being around each other leads.

Just skip the restaurant-and-theater-tickets drill. The pressure of a big, fancy first date is best left to kids who haven't learned yet that it's overkill. If you meet someone who you think has potential, start modestly with lunch, or maybe coffee at a local cafe. Going to a lecture on a nearby campus? Ask if she'd like to come along, then suggest stopping for a piece of pie. You're most appealing when you're doing something you enjoy. Three rules: Be positive, talk about the future, and be curious about her. Resist making that joke about how awkward it is to be on a date after a zillion years—it's a clunker.

Now, you say you want to date again, "just for companionship." Does that mean you don't want love? Or sex? After all, those are two of the best incentive awards out there. Just be sure you're not aiming low because you assume they can't happen to you again, or because you fear dishonoring your late wife. "After a long, loving marriage, it's sometimes difficult to let go of your spouse," says Patti Britton, Ph.D., a sexologist in Los Angeles and expert for iVillage.com. That's why middle-aged men invent hundreds of lame reasons not to call back a perfectly charming woman. Stay open to the possibility of finding a soul mate for the third act of your life. It happens all the time!

**Q** I've been out of the dating game for quite a while. Three months ago I met a terrific man, and recently he asked me to go on a weekend trip with him. I want to be intimate with him, but it's been so long I'm not sure how my body has changed. I don't want this to be awkward.

**A** If you've been sexually inactive for a long time, or you've gone through menopause since your last relationship, you may find intercourse a little uncomfortable, says Jean Koehler, Ph.D., a past president of the American Association of Sex Educators, Counselors, and Therapists. A drop in your estrogen levels and decrease in lubrication often thin vaginal tissues—and can make sex slightly painful. Also, your sex drive and responsiveness may not be quite as powerful as they once were. A natural decrease in testosterone and estrogen can cause some women—though certainly not all—to have less sexual desire and to take a little longer to get aroused.

Your gynecologist can help with both of these issues. Topical lubricants can eliminate the unwanted sensitivity. Some women find that feminine botanical massage oils boost their sexual arousal; these are over-the-counter herbal remedies sold in health stores, and they are designed for direct genital application. For sexual healing, however, nothing beats making love. Once you start to have sex regularly, your body will adapt and begin functioning much as it did when you were more sexually active, says Koehler.

##### Love in the
## LATE AFTERNOON

**H**istory abounds with famous lovers who out-romanced Casanova well into their later years. In 1834, for example, 30-year-old baroness Aurore Dupin impulsively abandoned her husband of nine years and their quiet French country life for the excitement of literary Paris. There she adopted masculine dress—trousers, top hats, ties—and a masculine nom de plume: George Sand. The conversion transformed her love life as well: For the next 23 years, Sand had affairs with the leading men of her day, including composer Frédéric Chopin. In her 70s, she enjoyed an intense relationship with novelist Gustave Flaubert.

If Paris is for lovers, age is no impediment to getting your groove on in the city of lights. As a 40-year-old American expatriate, outré author Henry Miller met a fellow bon vivant, Anaïs Nin, and made her the lust of his life. Nin inspired many of the sexually explicit passages that got Miller's *Tropic of Cancer* and *Tropic of Capricorn* banned in the United States. Returned stateside, Miller married five times (the last at age 62) and settled in Big Sur, California, where he permitted his fondness for nude Ping-Pong to be captured on film.

Another pioneer of later-life sexuality was Mae West. In 1926, her Broadway farce *Sex* landed the 34-year-old West in jail for eight days on obscenity charges—after the show's 375th performance. Indeed, West's brazenly sexual persona became her claim to fame. She ad-libbed her signature line—"Is that a sword in your pocket, or are ya pleased to see me?"—at age 52, when a fellow actor in the 1944 stage comedy *Catherine Was Great* walked on stage holding a prop at a suggestive angle.

In her 60s, West headlined Vegas revues filled with well-oiled musclemen. One of them, bodybuilder Paul Novak, became West's lover and companion. Though more than 30 years her junior, Novak stayed by her side until she died at 88. "Those who are easily shocked," West purred, "should be shocked more often." —ANDY STEINER

Realize that your partner may harbor similar worries, and you can help put him at ease. "It makes sense to be less intercourse-focused than perhaps you were in the past," advises Koehler. "The hands and mouth are very sexual." Include condoms in the fun—the number of reported sexually transmitted infections (STIs) in women above 50 has been on the rise, so don't think safe sex is the exclusive concern of bed-hopping twentysomethings.

Before you get busy at all, however, you'd be smart to discuss what taking the sexual step means to both of you. "Does it imply commitment? Exclusivity? These are important questions," says Koehler. It may not be necessary that you see it precisely the same way, but if you've been out of the sexual whirl for a while, it makes sense to know what you're getting into other than satin sheets.

**Q** For the past seven years, I have been deeply in love with a 75-year-old man (I'm 45, with a 14-year-old son and a 10-year-old daughter from my first marriage). We've been engaged for the last three years, but my fiancé does not want to discuss the "M" word. After making plans to visit Australia, he was disappointed to learn I do not want to go with him. I believe in marriage, and I believe I need to model values and morals for my kids.

My fiancé and I are soul mates, and I love him passionately. However, he has decided to take his 72-year-old married sister on the trip—without her husband. Is that normal?

Why can't I get the love of my life to commit to marriage? He thinks it's fine to go through life without being married, and he doesn't understand the responsibility I feel to be a role model for my children. Please advise.

**A** You want to travel with a husband, not a fiancé. You want to set a moral tone for your children, but he doesn't want to marry you. And you think traveling with his sister seems weird, yet he's taking her anyway.

So… I confess I'm perplexed: Exactly how do you define "soul mate"? Finding a fantastic person who is terrific to be with does not automatically translate into a loving husband—or, in your case, into the package deal of loving husband and stepfather.

I wonder if you have become so infinitely adaptable, in an attempt to stay connected to him, that you are stretched like a Gumby doll. You may be soul mates, but your heart must finish what you started before you met him. Your first commitment must be to your children—raising them until they are solidly launched in life.

As you point out, you view life quite differently from the vantage point of 45 than he does from 75. But this isn't an age difference, it's a time warp. For all the overlap that currently exists in your lives, you may as well have been born in different centuries. At a time in your life when you are up to your eyebrows in commitments to others, your fiancé will commit only to himself. It seems that you are asking if fun, friendship, and passion translate into "I do," "I care about you and your kids," and "I will adapt to the needs of others." The answer is that they don't—and that, frankly, he won't.

When the reluctant gentleman shoves off for Australia, tell him to do likewise. It will be sad and you will grieve. But knowing when to say "Enough!" is the first step in understanding your values. It is also the best role model you could ever give two impressionable young children.

**Q** After my divorce I met a wonderful man—a widower 10 years older than me—and we got engaged. He passed away last year. I'm still heartbroken, but I have resolved to get on with my life and finish my education. Because I think I'll never find anyone like him again, I'm more or less reconciled to being single forever. How do shy people like me put faith in the prospect of finding love again, when they're too shy to make it happen?

**A** Being shy can be a problem—unless you have moxie.

You've survived divorce and death; a lot of loss. At the time of your divorce, I wonder if you thought that love still lay somewhere ahead on the road of life. Then you met your wonderful man, and took a risk, loved, and lost him. Now you face that road again, and it is lonelier than it was before. You'll need all the nerve you can summon up to walk down it.

You are wisely reconnecting with other interests. For starters, you will never regret getting your education! And you should also be aware that being heartbroken is the natural result of having a heart you were willing to open and share. But deciding to be single "forever" sounds more like a defense against further heartbreak than a true resolution. So maybe your moxie is just in need of a little healing.

In my mind, grief is like those Russian nesting dolls. Each doll opens to reveal another doll inside, its every detail intricately rendered. Because you never know when you may have reached the last, each new discovery must be grieved: You break it apart, and out comes yet another memory of loss. The loss can hurt so much that you retreat, even from feeling the pain of grief. But be reassured that facing grief brings forward movement, however grind-ingly slow it may occur. This takes time. It will also take stamina.

Try not to confuse the pain of your grief with your per-sonality characteristics. Right now your job is to grieve. From your description above—and to your great credit—it's clear that you have not permitted your shyness to insulate you from relationships. Nor have you let it undermine your resolution to move forward, nor your determination to accomplish things for yourself. When it comes to faith in the future, that's what courage always leads to—and you've got courage.

**Q** Where do you go at age 50 and greater to find love, relationships, companionship, and romance?

**A** I suggest you begin with those interests that give you the greatest pleasure. What do you absolutely love to do in life? Where do you feel the most vibrant and alive? Which sports, games, hobbies, activities, or pastimes engage you so fully that you forget—at least for a moment—all about love, relationships, and romance?

That is your starting point. If these places or undertak-ings are lacking from your life, it's high time you developed a set of interests that bring you pleasure—and about which you feel passionate. Meaningful relationships happen when people feel they are of value, and that their lives are worth sharing with others.

So if you want romance, rent a 1940s musical on DVD or read one of the loftier novels by Jane Austen, such as *Emma* or *Pride and Prejudice*.

For companionship, however, nothing beats hanging out with good friends. And because this next bit of advice can never be adequately emphasized, allow me to repeat it here in slightly different form than I phrased it above: Relationships grow organically between two people who discover that they share a common connection or interest. Some relationships are fleeting; others take time to develop but are worth the wait. When you become so engrossed in life that you stop looking for love, that's when you'll find it.

**Q** I may be meeting a man in person very soon whom I currently know only through telephone (business) contact. I have had some very nice conversations with him on the phone. However, I have not "dated" for many years, and am somewhat insecure about how to behave. I have been "myself" on the phone with him, and we seemed compatible that way. He is divorced and lives alone, whereas my thirty-something son lives with me (not I with him). Any hints, advice, or suggestions?

**A** Unless you plan to conduct a perpetual telephonic romance, you two will need to meet. Why not invite him for coffee? Keep it low-key: Drive your own car, meet at a public place at the end of a workday, and talk. If you're comfortable and all goes well, the two of you will decide to meet again. Keep this up for a while, vary the venue, et voilà—you're dating!

Chances are good that at some point he'll say, "Your place or mine?"—and he won't be referring to a home-cooked meal. You'll need to level with him that you have a housemate. If he comes to your house, that will give you a chance to watch him interact with your son—vital information in the dating world. Most people want to date only those who are nice to their friends and family members. If you want privacy, of course, go to his place, not yours.

I can think of a dozen reasons why your son might still be living with you—some honorable and worth preserving, others codependent and in need of change. If you're unhappy with having your son at home, why not use this opportunity to revamp your living situation? Then you too can say, "Your place or mine all mine?"

**Q** I'm a good guy and a great father. I also happen to be an ex-convict. That was 27 years ago, and I've had no problems since. I'm single and want to be honest. How and when should I reveal it?

**A** There's a strong case for not revealing it until a relationship starts to show long-term potential. "There ought to be a statute of limitations on how long ex-prisoners need to identify themselves to strangers and new acquaintances," says Shadd Maruna, author of *Making Good: How Ex-Convicts Reform and Rebuild Their Lives*.

Once dating morphs into something more serious, however, disclosure is necessary (and, of course, it's best to err on the early side if your crime was violent). Try to turn honesty about your past—and your concern for her feelings—into pluses. In a quiet and public place, try this: "I'm so enthused about getting to know you, I think there's something you should know about me. I hope it won't upset you, but I'll understand if it does. When I was a much younger man, I was in prison."

Tell her exactly what you did. Answer all of her questions. Stress that you've put this behind you. Make it clear that you'll understand if she no longer wants to date. If she doesn't take it well, maybe she'll soften as the shock recedes.

# 2

# Dating Etiquette

**Q** I want to use a personal ad to find a man—for dates and maybe traveling. A friend's ad said she wanted a "companion," but the men she met wanted more. How can I avoid meeting weirdos?

**A** A lot of people want to barge into your life (and your bed) before the waiter brings the check these days, but it's better to take it easy and see if your hearts spark.

Before placing an ad, try the old-fashioned approach. "Personal ads are a great way to meet others, but often people jump right to them without putting themselves in circulation in their community," says Steve Nakamoto, who wrote *Men Are Like Fish: What Every Woman Needs to Know About Catching a Man*. Meeting men through a dinner club or a charity will let you assess them in a casual setting and thus avoid a lot of awkward coffee chats.

If you take out an ad, be clear. "Paint a word picture of exactly what you're looking for," says Laurence Minsky, coauthor of *25 Words or Less: How to Write Like a Pro to Find That Special Someone through Personal Ads*. "If you're not interested in romance, say precisely that—but then describe what you do want." Work in a few key buzzwords: You want friendship with a movie-and-coffee buddy, or a traveling sidekick for good dinner conversation. Strike "companionship"; it has sexual suggestions. Trite scribbles such as "moonlit walks" or "looking for fun" can also convey the wrong hints. Read the local personals to spot other clichés to avoid. Your ad may get fewer replies than a more provocative one would, but you won't be bothered by every presumptuous guy with a prescription for the latest erectile enhancer burning a hole in his pocket.

**Q** Since my divorce 12 years ago, I've had my fair share of dates. Then, through the Internet personals a couple of months back, I finally met a man I had absolute chemistry with. He seemed to feel it too, but after just a couple of weeks he started to back off.

The last time I saw him—over a month ago—it was wonderful! He seemed just as bubbly and thrilled as I was.

Now I feel like I don't know what's going on. I'm not sure if I should just ask him that question point-blank, or whether

I should even contact him. John Gray's Mars/Venus book says I shouldn't take the initiative—that I should wait for him to contact me. What do you think?

**A** It is dumfounding to establish a great connection with someone only to have him vanish into thin air. It makes you doubt your assessment skills.

For some people, being thrilled and bubbly can mean they harbor a very deliberate desire to get closer to others—to establish intimacy, to find a partner for life. Other people—no matter how effervescent they may appear in the moment—possess an equally intense desire to stay free of all encumbrances. Still others delight in making the sort of sparkling connection you describe, then mysteriously disappear at evening's end. This third group contains what I like to think of as the unstable isotopes of the dating world: They're good for only one brief chemical bond at a time.

If you ask me—and you did—I think it's fine to contact The Invisible Man and ask him point-blank why he seems to go as fast in reverse as he does in forward. See if he can explain this behavior to your satisfaction. Only then can you truly find out if what you had still sizzles—or has fizzled.

Dating in midlife is remarkably (some would say "disturbingly") reminiscent of dating in adolescence. As in the scandalously inequitable social scene that prevailed in your teenage years, it seems that everyone but you has found a partner—even though you personally would not be interested in half of them. You're single, you're lonely, you're discouraged (I know this because I hear it detailed in my office). You can't quite divine the "rules of engagement," yet you don't have a lifetime to waste in figuring them out.

The difference between 50 and 15 is that you now know who you are. However vulnerable or tired you may feel, you've seen yourself through plenty of ups and downs. If things don't work out with this guy—if his constantly running hot and cold makes you feel tapped out—keep experimenting with other elements. As in the ballroom (or bedroom!), practice makes perfect in the laboratory of life.

**Q** Several of my friends are very into Internet dating, but I'm a little wary of meeting people this way. Do you have any suggestions for how to screen dates?

**A** Your uneasiness makes sense: We're used to sizing up people through all kinds of verbal and visual clues you can't get from a computer screen. Also, cyber-Romeos don't have a seal of approval—as in, he's a friend of your sister's masseuse—and that makes the terrain even trickier.

However, established online dating services (Match.com, Matchmaker.com, etc.) keep your e-mail address confidential and take other steps to screen out creeps. With a few smart precautions, you may actually find invitations by computer preferable to meeting strangers in smoky bars.

First, stay anonymous for as long as you feel comfortable doing so, regardless of the other person's questions. Don't reveal any identifying details about yourself until you're satisfied that Damon from Dayton is the Nobel laureate he says he is. If you feel pressured, don't hesitate to end the connection. "You should be less concerned for other people's feelings than for your own safety," says Trish McDermott, vice president at Match.com. "The beauty of this technology is that you can just cut the line and cast again."

Does that strike you as rude? Don't sweat it. It's accepted etiquette in online dating.

Request a *recent* picture. No, you can't judge a book by its cover, but you can judge a person who can't use a comb. "Good online dating sites make it easy to send a picture," says McDermott. "Reluctance to do so is a red flag."

Third, watch for even small inconsistencies in the messages. Did your online suitor graduate from Ohio University or Ohio State? If he's lying in his notes, he'll likely contradict himself at some point. If possible, verify your correspondent's marital status; sad to say, not everyone is as legally available as they may represent themselves.

If you decide to meet, use blind-date common sense: Choose a crowded public place, and transport yourself to and from the date. If he seems like a prize catch who deserves a second date, go for it. But remember Reagan's slogan regarding Soviet disarmament: Trust but verify.

**Q** A friend and I have decided to go on a cruise. The cruise line advertises that it attracts "single people of all ages," and other friends have had wonderful times. We thought this might be a fun way to meet some active men who like to travel. Any tips?

**A** First, make sure the cruise will have the kind of passengers you're hoping for. I'd be wary of those aimed at "single people of all ages," even if your friends have had terrific times. You don't want to be surrounded by twenty-somethings doing body shots. "Ask the booking agent specific questions about the average age of the people on the cruise," suggests Erik Elvejord, public relations director for Holland America cruises. A tip: The longer and costlier the cruise, the more passengers you'll see of your own age. Ask about the gender breakdown on board, too. You're less likely to find Mr. World Traveler if 80 percent of your shipmates are women.

Find the ship's social hostess and cruise director as soon as you board and tell them you'd enjoy meeting other singles. "They're the key people to meet," says Martin Lilly, entertainment director of Cunard Line. They'll steer you to the right parties (there may be a shindig for solo travelers early in the cruise), lounges, activities, and day trips where you can meet other singles. Also, ask the maitre d' of the ship's dining room to seat you with other solo travelers.

Finally, pack your dancing shoes. "If you're a good dancer," says Elvejord, "you'll be much in demand."

**Q** I met someone in Hawaii in 2003. I was very attracted to him, and we went to dinner three evenings in a row (he was tied up teaching during the day). He then went home to another island, and I went home at the end of my vacation.

We e-mailed each other every couple of weeks or so for the next six months. Early in 2004, I saw him on another island—same situation, except that I was staying at a place far from the school where he teaches. So he offered his place, no strings attached. I accepted—and very much enjoyed his company in the evenings.

I have wanted to live in Hawaii for more than 30 years, and as a registered nurse I should be able to find work there fairly easily. One of my two daughters, however, clearly does not want me to move there. "It's too far away," she objects.

## Screening Your Callers
# WHEN DATING ONLINE

When education professor Louise Jacobsen married for the second time, she figured she could mothball her dating skills for good. Two years later, her husband was dead from pancreatic cancer and Jacobsen was a widow at 54. Urged by a friend to try online dating, Jacobsen joined both Match.com and eHarmony.com. "It seemed like a quick way to meet 10 people and find one I clicked with," she says.

Jacobsen had no problem attracting cybersuitors—a testament to the exploding popularity of online dating among older Americans. According to Nielsen/NetRatings Inc., an Internet research firm, more than 16 percent of those who belong to the five most popular dating websites are 55 and older. "Online dating is a new social phenomenon," says Andrea Orr, author of *Meeting, Mating (…and Cheating): Sex, Love, and the New World of Online Dating.* "A lot of older Americans have moved to new cities or are physically limited. Online dating allows them to be social from their living rooms."

But isn't online dating, with its potential for creeps and liars, a dangerous gamble? Not if you follow a few safety guidelines, says Orr: "Protect yourself by setting up an online account that doesn't use your real name. Devise a screen name that doesn't reveal much, such as 'Joe in Oklahoma City.'" Whenever Jacobsen met an e-mail date in person, she checked in with a friend before and after. "But I was never afraid," she says. "We always met in neutral territory."

Heed your instincts about the people you encounter, says Orr. Jacobsen believed mutual interests were key to potential compatibility, so she never included a photo with her profile—an unpopular decision. "I met one guy who was funny and had similar interests. We flirted a lot by e-mail—we even hit it off in person." Just as the relationship picked up steam, however, Jacobsen met another man offline who shared her field of work and loved spending time with her grandchildren. She's been with him ever since.  —ELIZABETH LARSEN

My island love is well-established there, and does not want to move away from his (married) daughter.

Never have I felt so happy and complete. Six days together, one visit to his daughter's home, four or five phone calls, and several e-mails—can this be real? We both weathered two unsuccessful marriages in our 20s and have remained single since then, working and parenting. Both of my daughters truly want me to be happy. I would probably sell my home and resign my present position. Your thoughts?

**A** You're excited about living in Hawaii, but pause to consider what "Aloha" might ultimately entail for you:

**A** *Ask* yourself: How many friends have bought timeshares while vacationing in Cancun, only to regret being carried away by the moment? How many return from a trip to the islands intent on going back—then decide to go to Europe instead the following year?

**L** *Love* demands much more than a handful of e-mails and phone calls and a few agreeable evenings. Does the term "moon glow" resonate with you? It's an old-fashioned term meaning "the moon casts spells on the unsuspecting"—quite applicable, I think, in your case.

**O** *Once* upon a time…. All fairy tales sound so full of promise at the beginning, don't they? Step back from the story you have spun, however, and weigh some of the hard realities that may lie behind the myth. Were you to slip and break a leg, for example, what would life be like without your current network of friends to support you?

**H** *Home* is where the heart is, so have him visit yours, meet your friends there, and spend time with your daughters. Island Boy needs to get a vivid sense of what your world is like in order to understand what you are leaving behind. This may be why your daughter, who obviously wants you to be happy, also wants you to slow down.

**A** *Always* leave yourself escape routes. If you decide to move, rent your house rather than selling it, and request a leave from work rather than quitting outright. In other words, don't erase your current life; instead, put it on hiatus.

One thing is clear: You need a challenging new adventure that will tap your considerable energies, talents, and emotions. Feeling swept away is part of a really good vacation— just don't let it sweep away your judgment.

**Q** The man I'm seeing asked me to go with him on a European vacation. I said yes, but he hasn't said a word about who's paying the expenses. I can't afford to pay half of everything, but I don't want to assume that he's covering it all. How do I bring this up and what should I suggest?

**A** Swallow your pride and use this script: "Bill, I'm embarrassed about something. My enthusiasm about our vacation got ahead of my wallet, and I realize I just can't afford the trip." If he offers to pay your way, simply decide whether or not to accept his generosity. If you do, problem solved. But if you're uneasy about it, thank him and say that you'd like to pay for the expenses you can afford. Perhaps you could suggest that you pay your airfare and, after the trip, you'll treat him to some home-cooked meals, to thank him for picking up your accommodations.

If he doesn't volunteer to pay for any costs, you still have options. Mr. Credit Card could be a reasonable fix. (Some opportunities in life are worth taking on a little credit card debt, so long as you're in good financial shape otherwise.) Second, you could propose a more modest vacation. Who needs Athens? You can have a wonderful and cheaper time together in Yellowstone National Park or a bed-and-breakfast nestled in the nearest mountain range.

**Q** I'm dating a woman with a 14-year-old daughter who accompanies us everywhere. The daughter is disrespectful to me by blasting music and otherwise acting out. I've asked her mother to step in, but it hasn't helped. What can I do?

**A** The terms of the mother-daughter deal were laid down long before you showed up. If Mom lets her blare music or otherwise behave obnoxiously, she's a doormat parent who needs her daughter's approval more than she needs you.

"The mother needs to make maturity demands of her daughter but still acknowledge her daughter's discomfort with a new man in her mom's life," says Christy Buchanan, Ph.D., coauthor of *Adolescents After Divorce*. To ease this transition, try to carve out more time for the relationship that doesn't include the daughter, Buchanan advises. This is deep water, but gently suggest that now and then she not be included in your plans. This will get the relationship out of her face for a while. Meanwhile, it's her mother's responsibility to get to the root of this.

In the short term, you're not going to teach the daughter the rules of polite society. For your own sanity, consider making a goodwill gesture. Ask her about the music with which she's damaging your hearing, and the next day show up with the group's latest CD, and a house gift, too: the headphones that would allow domestic tranquillity.

# 3

# What's Age Got To Do with It?

**Q** For the past several months I have been developing a relationship with the most wonderful man. We have excellent conversation. There seems to be a fiery chemistry. In fact, we seem outrageously compatible.

I do have one major concern, though: I am 56, and he is 45. Although he says this is not an issue, I'm afraid it may become one at some point. (I thought he was older; he thought I was younger.)

I did not purposely seek out a younger man, nor did he go looking for an older woman. He is talking of marriage later on, but I am just not sure. I am concerned, and because of that I hold back. He, on the other hand, does not hold back: He treats me with such love and talks excitedly about our future life together.

Some of my friends say I'm nuts. They say I should "go for the gusto" and just be happy as long as possible.

What do you think?

**A** I think your "fiery chemistry" and "outrageous compatibility" are a foolproof recipe for fun, and that your friends are giving you good advice.

I know this relationship is new and that you may still be "high on love," but here are some things to look forward to if you stay with this guy:

Dating younger men is all the rage. You'll be the neighborhood pacesetter. A 2004 AARP survey of the sexual mores of older Americans reported that 34 percent of single women over 40 are dating younger men.

No one can trap you in a conversation about how all the guys in their 50s have aged so much less gracefully than the women. You can be the first one on your block to put that trash talk on the curb!

The kicker: Because women live seven years longer than men, on average, you stand a good chance of checking out from planet Earth at roughly the same time. Talk about an exit strategy!

But what about the pain, you say? Shouldn't we address the prospect of emotional suffering? Sure, he could leave you—but you might just as easily tire of him. Rapport unravels and bonds dissolve with no regard for age differences.

Yes, the thoughtless and the malcontent will throw their unfair share of ageist comments your way. But be an activist and set them straight: When a woman says, "He's just dating you until someone his own age comes along," fire right back with, "Unless I drop him first!" If she snorts, "Give me a guy I can count on—one my own age," dish out a little reality in return: "Count on to do what—die?"

But what about a truly ugly moment—one where a supposedly nice guy suggests your beau's attraction to you is based on his own feelings of inferiority? Treat his vindictiveness with veniality: Pat his knee, flash your biggest smile, and sashay off with your trendsetter.

Naysayers aside, the deepest pitfalls may be those that pockmark memory lane. You grew up with Captain Kangaroo; he's a fan of Scooby-Doo. You had ears only for Mickey; he leaped around like Spider-Man. Your screen pals were Howdy Doody, Buffalo Bob, and Clarabelle; his were Rocky, Bullwinkle, and Boris & Natasha. Things could be even more chronologically chronic, of course; what if you'd fallen in love with a South Park fan?

Despite your reluctance and his impulsiveness, you have joyful hearts and compatible personalities. For that reason alone, I foresee no star-crossed twists of fate in your destiny together.

**Q** I'm in my 70s and have been seeing a man who is in his early 60s. I'm sure he knows that I am older than he is, but I don't think he knows how much (I look younger than my age, but it's more than 10 years higher than his). We just don't talk about it. I would never lie to him, but what do I say if he ever asks?

**A** Would never lie to him? You *are* lying to him. Who cares if you've never actually uttered words that are untrue? Letting him assume you're younger than you are is a lie. A court of law might acquit you of perjury, but you're still guilty. This is no way to run a relationship. Besides, unless he's completely asleep at the switch—or you're a world-class knockout—he already knows how old you are, give or take a couple of years. He can't be that stupid. I would bet he senses quite clearly that you want to avoid talking about the age difference between the two of you—and that he is graciously accommodating your wishes.

You're the one who's losing here. Trying not to expose your lie will only put more nervous pressure on you the longer it goes on, and it'll become harder and harder to cover your tracks, so to speak. How long can you date a person without reminiscing about your childhood during some incidental conversation? Where will you set it—during the Depression or the postwar prosperity? If you think you'll simply continue to avoid all topics that might give a clue about your model year, you won't be sharing much of yourself with this man. Your interaction may start to feel a little superficial after a while. And he won't be to blame.

Don't wait for him to ask your age; reveal it as soon as possible. Talk about hearing the news about Pearl Harbor when you were in school. Women lying about—excuse me, obscuring—how old they are is a deeply sexist practice in that it's motivated by the thought that, when it comes to womenfolk, younger is better. That's not true. In the slim chance that he loses interest in you because you're older than he thought, he's a fool—and best ousted sooner rather than later.

## Falling in
# LUST AGAIN

After escaping a bad 20-year marriage, Joyce Nelson was resigned to a life sans romance. "I didn't think I would ever be attracted to a man again—or one to me."

A few years after her divorce, Nelson ventured into online dating. She traded e-mails and phone calls with a few men, but no sparks flew. Then she got a message from 62-year-old widower Bruce Shellhart. Heartened by some lively phone banter, Nelson agreed to meet him for dinner. The meal lasted three hours.

Alone at home that evening, Nelson realized she was strongly attracted to Shellhart. "I hadn't felt those stomach butterflies since I was 16." As they spent more time together, the couple found they'd both been in a dry spell: Shellhart's wife had died after a lengthy illness, and sex had been just another chore in Nelson's marriage.

All that soon changed—and Nelson couldn't keep her sexual reawakening a secret. "The phone would ring and I'd get all giddy and giggly," she recalls. "My daughters, in their late teens and early 20s, would roll their eyes and say, 'Mom, that's so gross!'"

Richard Carroll, director of the sex and marital therapy program at Northwestern University Medical School, says sex between mature lovers can be particularly satisfying. "There's an understanding of physical limitations and imperfections, a sense of gratitude and wonder that can make the sex very satisfying."

Eventually, Nelson and Shellhart married. They merged families, then moved in with Shellhart's 95-year-old mother after she broke her hip. That arrangement can rein in intimacy ("Her hearing is better than we'd like," Nelson jokes), yet the couple still can't keep their hands off each other—a fact that makes Nelson smile.

"My grandma once said, 'Inside this old woman is a 16-year-old girl who knows what it was like to be kissed for the first time.' I finally understand how she felt. The amazing thing is that it feels even better now than it did then." —ANDY STEINER

**Q** **FROM PERSON A:** How does a 60-year-old woman who looks 45 find love?

I am a professional artist and educator, and a bilingual widow who has lived and worked in different countries and states. My grown children live in other countries; most of them are professionals, with families of their own. I just can't seem to find Mr. Right—and I have tried. Blind dates, Internet dating, men I've met on my own—all have been dating disasters. Most of the men I meet by chance are too young, yet the men my age strike me as too old.

I don't want to spend the rest of my life alone, as my 80-year-old mother and 59-year-old sister (both divorced) seem destined to, but I'm getting to the point where I won't go out alone anymore. Friends my age are married and don't like to go anywhere.

**Q** **FROM PERSON B:** I am a male in his mid-60s, a non-smoker, and a social drinker. I have a very athletic appearance from jogging and working out at a local gym on a daily basis. I ride a motorcycle, but am not a biker; I also have a private pilot's license.

I have no interest in living the lifestyle of an older person. I identify primarily with younger people and activities. So how do I meet younger women?

**A** Person B, does the vanity plate on the back of your Harley read "NRCSST"?

Person A, allow me to introduce you to Person B. The two of you have so much in common:

1) You both look and act (by your own accounts) much younger than your 60+ years.

2) You are both hyper out the wazoo. The ideal soul mate for each of you is obviously going to be someone for whom instant gratification takes too long. Person B, perhaps you could put that private pilot's license to good use by ferrying Person A from one foreign country to the next on her "Flying Grannies 2005 World Tour." And Person A, perhaps you could put your artistic endowments to equally productive use by air-brushing some gaudy artwork on Person B's motorcycle. I suggest something tasteful and socially redeeming, such as a nude pose of the two of you flexing your respective immaculate buffness.

3) Like Egyptian crocodiles, you are both deep in denial about your age. I suggest you get together at Person B's La Jolla townhouse or Person A's Miami Beach condo (I'm guessing) to swap reminiscences about how you got carded the last time—two weeks ago—you bought fine wine. Best of all, this arrangement will obviate that bothersome need of venturing out alone to beard those thirty- and fortysomethings in their lions' den.

Should your hankering to drop in on those "wild things" prove unquenchable, however, this is where and when you will find them:

*Weekdays 8-5:* Work

*Weekdays 5-12:* Work at home, aka homework (with their kids)

*Weekends 8-5:* Soccer fields, high schools, college campuses (with their kids)

*Weekends 5-12:* Fast asleep in front of a rented video (and wondering where their kids are, and who they're with)

But don't let the facts dissuade you. Just wait a few years and they'll be 60, too. Meanwhile, introduce yourself to the people around you—the real people you actually come in contact with—and try going out with them. And who knows? Just because you don't act your age doesn't mean you can't date it!

**Q** I have been a widow for about one year. A few months after my husband passed away, I met a widower whose wife had died roughly the same number of months before. He is nine years my senior and retired; I still have 11 years to go before I retire. He is an empty nester; I still have two sons (ages 18 and 22) in my household.

He and I started dating, and now we have become intimate. I have not introduced him to my family because I don't think my sons are ready to meet him. He agrees that my sons are unprepared for such a development.

When I was living as a single mom in the past, I never introduced my sons to the men I dated—until I met my (now-deceased) husband. By the time my sons met him, he and I both knew our relationship would be permanent.

My relationship with my new beau is a shared oasis from the desert of our separate grief. I love his company and he loves mine. He is charming and handsome, and I respect his wisdom and experience.

I can feel him holding back, though. He has no responsibilities—nor (with respect to my sons) does he want any. For their part, I don't think they would accept a new father figure at their age. I understand and accept that the few years I have left with my sons is my responsibility—one that I both cherish and dread now that my husband is dead.

Given our age difference, what are the possibilities for a future with my widower friend?

**A** I enthusiastically encourage you to keep guiding and supporting your sons, but I have to ask you this: Why do you feel the dread of responsibility? It's almost certain that your sons—now young adults—will not respond to your friend as they did to their stepfather. They have moved beyond the point of looking for a father, but they would probably welcome some unvarnished adult friendship and caring. They may actually be worried about your loneliness and your well-being. If that's the case, think how reassured they might be to know that you are finding new friendships in your new life.

Now here comes the tough-love part of today's proceedings: Is your real concern that your relationship with this man—which you have carefully kept isolated from other aspects of your life—will not mesh well with your continuing responsibilities to your family and work? The demands that you have allowed your sons to make on your time may conflict with this tender new part of your life. Brutally put, you're overmothering all three of these men.

This situation calls for the sort of clarity not routinely found in crystal balls. You can't keep these two facets of your personal life segregated indefinitely. You and your friend need to discuss the present, not the future: Acknowledge that your sons are young men to whom you are mother—but for whom he will never be father (nor should he ever try to be).

This is one case where the path through the relationship jungle is clearly defined—and unequivocally labeled: It reads, "Plain Speaking" and "Careful Planning." With your two sons now at voting age and beyond, your days as the Brady Bunch are (blissfully, I hope) behind you.

**Q** I am in my early 60s. I am slim and attractive, with (I like to flatter myself) a good personality, but I find the singles scene so frustrating! There are quite a few places to go and things to do for women in their 30s, 40s, & 50s, but once you hit 60 it's like you've contracted some sort of disease!

For a while I thought it was just me, and I couldn't figure out what was wrong. (No one would mistake me for 45, but I like to have fun, and I have a good attitude about life in general.) This week, however, I realized it isn't just me—it's the generation of older men, most of them aged 60 to 75, who seem to be living an illusion.

These guys do everything imaginable to avoid being near any woman over 55, lest it "spoil their image." If you say "Hello" to them, they don't react—some gal from 28 to 40 might notice and decide they're not desirable. They swagger up and flirt with these young women, who resent their attention but consent to talk with them rather than sit alone.

These older men—who can't even begin to keep up with me and quite a few women I know—deceive themselves into thinking these younger women will fall for them. They need to wake up to the fact that women closer to their age would make great companions: We wouldn't make them look so ridiculous, and the loneliness they must feel would disappear.

While the men our age are out making fools of themselves, a lot of us have to say "Thanks, but no thanks!" to men 80 years old and up.

Us gals are tired of being frustrated! How can we get this message across?

**A** You're right as rain, but don't hold your breath waiting for this cohort to get with the program.

You want to get your message across, but which abyss are you talking about—the age divide, the gender divide, the marketing-to-youth divide, or the portrayal-in-media divide? Ageism is one of those peculiar growths that plague modern American life. Pair it with its evil twin—sexism—and you've got a powerful formula for the kind of dismissal and invisibility you've been experiencing.

Ageism and sexism are complex noxious organisms. They are rooted in self-hatred (on the part of older guys), they thrive on ignorance (all those young people behind the cosmetic counters), and they spread thanks to social anxiety (just about everybody else who needs educating). Throw in the baser aspects of human nature—such as the desire to feel included by excluding others—and you've got more prejudice and intolerance than exists in any social situation outside the average middle school.

So what exactly can you do about it?

*Speak out.* When you're treated invisibly or disdainfully, do not go silent into that good night. The only folks you'll offend by calling attention to the slight are those you wouldn't want as friends in any event. They may not change their beliefs, but they'll watch their Ps and Qs whenever you (or someone like you) are around. Activism—which I define as speaking up for what you believe is right, and speaking up when you believe you've been wronged—is a cornerstone not just of citizenship but of adulthood itself. Never is it needed more vitally than when clueless adults are doing their knuckleheaded thing. If that older gent who dissed you had spinach stuck in his teeth, you'd tell him so. If he's acting pathetic, give him a shot at redemption.

*Move out.* If you're hanging out with superficial people, find a different group—one that values substance over appearance. You already know who these people are, because once upon a time you sought them out in order to survive high school and college. Stop strolling the board-walk and get on a board—a skateboard, a surfboard, a board of directors. Join activities that involve all levels of athleti-cism, art, and intellectual curiosity.

*Wait it out.* You've been hearing this your whole life, and it's true: The Baby Boomers—that elephant in the demographic python—are headed your way, and they are bringing reinforcements to your embattled ranks. When they arrive, their sheer numbers should help get the mes-sage across.

Social rifts and chasms don't heal overnight. But just as assuredly as you have a right to your rage, you have a right to a vibrant social life at 60 and beyond. So step out with others—and act as outrageous as you feel!

# Making Love

*Sex is one of the nine
reasons for reincarnation…
The other eight are unimportant.*
—HENRY MILLER

# Making Love

WHETHER YOU ARE SOLO or in a partnership, your sex life has potential—as long as you have the motivation. I'll always be grateful to the client who put it all in perspective: "Why care about sex? Because it's about the quality of your life. If you're living, you're interested in loving."

At the University of Michigan Sexual Health Counseling Services, where I practice, the average age of those seeking sex therapy is about 53. Does this mean that Midwesterners are slow to build up a head of steam? Not quite. To me it's an affirmation that people everywhere are unwilling to give up on the pleasure of being sexual. The "appetitive drive" for sex, like that for food, is hardwired: It's with us from before we are born and it stays with us until we die. As long as interest prevails, there is the potential for the feelings and connections we associate with sexual pleasure.

If it seems, however, that the frolicking adventurous singles portrayed in *Sex in the City* seem to be getting all the good times, think again. The most frequent sexual activity is happening all around you—in bedrooms of married couples who know that putting time into sex gives life to living. In the highly regarded National Health Survey, researchers found that the average American couple was having sex about once a week. This figure includes just about every-body you know—the butcher, the baker, the scented candle maker. In my discussions with people, it appears that the most likely time to make love is Saturday night or Sunday morning (so now you know when not to call your friends).

Sex is about living well—and living healthy. A 2003 white paper by Planned Parenthood, "The Health Benefits of Sexual Expression," made it clear that a vibrant sex life is conducive to both physical and mental health. Research conducted by the University of Chicago in 1999, meanwhile, has established that people who have orgasms regularly may live up to three years longer than those who do not.

But you don't need professional organizations or university research departments to convince you, right? If you are not in sexual bliss, chances are it's because you've hit a problem you don't know how to repair.

When sex is going well, it might take up 5 percent of your thinking time. When sex slumps, it can ruin the better part of a day (or a relationship) with worry and resentment. What pulls the plug on passion or causes couples to roll away from their relationship? Aside from the physical things that can malfunction—the body is infinitely creative in this area—outside stressors, work overload, and relationship problems top the list of reasons why people get a headache. If sex has become all pain and no gain, or so predictable that channel surfing and shopping sprees create more pyrotechnics than the canoodling you've choreographed, it's time for a change. For some surefire ways to fire up your passion once again, read on.

# 4

# In the Bedroom

**Q** How do you teach a grown-up man to kiss? Through two marriages he never learned, or he's forgotten how. He gives me a peck on the lips, and that's about it.

**A** The kiss is perhaps the most underutilized skill in any man's sexual repertoire. And that's a pity, because his handicap is likely all in his head. "Most men who don't kiss were told somewhere along the line that they were bad at it," says Lou Paget, the female sex-expert author of *365 Days of Sensational Sex*. "It's a shame, because a man who's a good kisser will likely get all the sex he can handle."

If you want your man to pucker, be sure he knows that it's the gateway to greater glories. Once you've told him you really dig kissing, offer him a playful demonstration of what rings your bell, Paget says. In your sexiest tone, tell him there's something you'd like to show him—how you dream about being kissed. "Then kiss him exactly the way you wish he would kiss you. Ask him to imitate the kiss right back at you." If he does it right, tell him (and show him) you loved it. If he botches it, try another demonstration. Repeat as necessary.

**Q** I think good sex is much more than a matter of timing (that elusive goal of simultaneous orgasms). Equally outdated, in my mind, is the notion that sex is limited to intercourse; foreplay qualifies as sex just as much as copulation does. The word "foreplay" itself, in my opinion, betrays an obsolete understanding of human sexuality: It implies that foreplay is somehow a lesser part of sex than intercourse—a point of view held mostly by younger men.

Until the word "foreplay" is changed to something more descriptive or accurate, we will continue to labor under the assumption that foreplay is only an appetizer, whereas intercourse is the entree. Yet good, fulfilling sex should not be seen as a formal meal. It's more like a buffet, where each partner should feel free to select the items that appeal to her or him the most, and share them with his/her partner.

**A** Your position on this issue is absolutely correct, and you have argued it expertly. (Hey—you're not angling for my job, are you?)

**Q** Why is it that many men age 50 and above still enjoy sex as if they were 20 years old? My husband (to cite the sole source of my research) can still perform admirably, and he clearly enjoys sex very much. Is there a time in their life when this will lessen?

**A** The short but mostly accurate answer is "No." (Is that the answer you were hoping for?)

**Q** I really like intimacy, but my husband doesn't comprehend it—or its importance to our relationship. He also likes me to stimulate him orally, which I feel is unclean/unhealthy. Also, this becomes such a one-sided sexual encounter. Please address this issue for me (it causes many fights).

**A** Many couples find oral sex a normal and pleasurable part of sexual activity. The notion that genitals are dirty is just that—a myth and nothing more. Other parts of the body—the mouth, to cite an obvious example—harbor far more bacteria. Before lovemaking, many couples throw in a shower for good measure, leaving their bodies squeaky clean and ready for tasteful action. For sex to be mutually enjoyable, however, it must be a shared activity. This requires caring. This requires respect.

So… because this issue has become a bone of contention between the two of you, let me climb into the "ring of love" for a moment and take a turn as referee.

The rules are simple: Each erroneous belief articulated by either one of you will be branded as such by the sound of a gong. Any person receiving three chimes will be judged clueless and asked to leave the ring until he or she can prove they have listened to their partner—and wised up.

All right, now shake hands, return to your neutral corners, and hold forth on the state of your relationship!

"Being married relieves me of the obligation to understand the importance of intimacy."

*Gong!*

Marriage is built on a three-legged stool of friendship, love, and respect. If you value your wife as the lifelong friend she can and should be, you will want to figure out why she considers intimacy such a vital part of your relationship.

"A one-sided sexual encounter is fine, even when it involves asking someone to do something they're uncomfortable with."

*Gong, gong!*

Does the phrase "We've come a long way, baby!" mean nothing whatsoever to you? Treating a woman as if she is in servitude is not only archaic, it's downright dangerous. Is it possible some deep-seated problem is causing you to debase your wife in this way? Remember, there's a reason we call them conjugal—not subjugal—relations.

"We do it this way because we've always done it this way."

*Gong, gong, and gong again!* People who trot out this trope have discovered that an excess of mulishness may absolve them of the necessity to change. Beware: You may be on the verge of being "outstubborned" by your wife.

Sexuality is a potent force. It can be wondrous—spiritual, even—when a couple makes love to each other. But when one partner insists on acting insensitive or even cruel, sex can also be used to hurt or humiliate people. This is flat-out wrong. Tell your husband he won't "get lucky" again until

## The Joy of
# VINTAGE SEX

**I**n the movies, the red-hot lover is almost always young. More style than substance, he can achieve an erection faster than he can spell his name. But the ladies don't mind a bit: They line up outside his bedroom door. In the movies, they always leave satisfied.

So much for the fantasy. While youth may equal sex appeal in popular culture, the reality is that age has its advantages when it comes to sexual intimacy. "The average time it takes a man in his 20s to go from sexy thoughts to orgasm is just seven minutes," says Jay Lewkowitz, executive director of Oakton Place, an independent retirement center in Des Plaines, Illinois. "For a woman it is 22 minutes at the fastest. So for much of their lives, women and men are essentially running at different speeds. But as a man gets older, he needs longer, stronger stimulation to achieve an erection and orgasm. As they age, men and women start to get more in synch with each other. And that can lead to some very satisfying sex."

For women, life's later years can bring a sexual reawakening. "Postmenopausal women often become very sexual simply because they feel freer," says Lewkowitz. "They don't have to worry about pregnancy. They feel like they can do whatever they want." For Sarah, a 52-year-old Minnesotan, seeing the last of her three children head off to college really perked up her sex life. Because she now has more time—and an emptier house—she and her boyfriend are free to get intimate whenever the mood hits. "Sex is better now, no question," she says. "I'm not always thinking about the kids. We have more time to focus on each other and what makes us happy."

Are you in a relationship that's passed the test of time? "This may be the opportunity to explore things you were too uptight to talk about when you were younger," says Lewkowitz. "If you've had sex with someone for 35 years, you might feel a little safer telling them your fantasies. You know they won't run away screaming. Sexually speaking, you could be entering the time of your life." —ANDY STEINER he learns how to relate to you, your needs, and your approach to sexuality.

**Q** My husband says not enough; I say we do okay—and probably better than average. How many couples who have been married more than 35 years still have sex? How often do they have it? And do they need a pill to make it happen?

**A** Lots of people over 60 lead happy—that is to say, active and healthy—sex lives. Whether you yourself are doing okay or better than average is just fine too.

In fact, no one really knows what average is, because people over 60 are breaking the sexual sound barrier. Perhaps the most reliable data base on the sexual habits and behaviors of those 45+ is the one compiled by AARP from two sex surveys it conducted in 1999 and 2004, with the results published in its magazine and on its website. The surveys are scientific, meaning they used a randomly selected group that was balanced to statistically reflect the nation's racial and ethnic diversity.

It turns out you're in the lucky group; people with a regular sexual partner have more positive outlooks on life, are less likely to feel stressed out or depressed, and think sexuality is a critical part of a good relationship.

Let's examine some of those averages you asked about:

■ About 66 percent of those responding have a regular sex partner and have been with that person for 10 years or longer—not quite your 35 years, granted, but neither are these people still locked in first-kiss passion.

■ Sexual activity is alive—and thriving: Thirty-three percent engage in sexual intercourse once a week or more often. Fifty percent report engaging in sexual touching and caressing, and 66 percent kiss and hug on a regular basis.

■ Half of all respondents have a sexual thought, fantasy, or erotic dream at least once a week; 25 percent have these at least once a day.

■ The usual time of day for sex is evening (50 percent), but morning is the second favorite (33 percent). As people get older, they prefer that morning time to late-night sex.

■ Sixty-six percent of people discuss their sexual satisfaction with their partner. Fifty percent of respondents said they were satisfied with their sex lives, whereas 20 percent said they were not. Your husband in not an aberration (statistically, at any rate) because more men than women stated they were dissatisfied with sex.

■ People in long-term relationships were more satisfied with their sex lives than those not involved in such relationships.

By "a pill," I assume you're talking about one of the numerous medications that foil the activity of enzymes (phosphodiesterases, notably PDE5) that inhibit erection. These medicines help men with erectile dysfunction by increasing blood flow to the penis. Even with "the pill," however, sexual stimulation is needed for erection. Most of the 16 million men worldwide who use this kind of medication would gratefully say it has gotten them through some hard times.

You seem to be wondering, "Are we normal?"

"Normal" is an overrated state of affairs. "Average" is a mere starting point. A more pertinent and productive question might be, "What works best for us?"

**Q** My wife has no interest in achieving an orgasm (I have tried to please her for many years, yet she has no interest). She never uses the word "sex." If I show any interest in sex or even mention the word, she says, "That's all you ever think about!" Any sex act has always been 100 percent initiated by me.

Please tell me my wife is not normal (all women can't be this indifferent!). I have tried all the "nice" things; nothing works. I feel like I'm raping her. Recently I suggested hormone therapy, but she will not even consider it. Should I try to persuade her to go to a sex therapist?

**A** In an ideal world, a couple's sexual passions synch up. You and your wife have a less-than-ideal situation for you both. Although many women cannot imagine having sex without having an orgasm, it is true that some women are not interested in orgasm. The same is true of initiating, talking about, or even thinking about sex. For some people, the sex blip simply doesn't glow on their radar screens.

Why?

The reasons are as varied as the human condition itself. They may stem from socialization, lack of education, trauma, depression, relationship issues, physical changes, or current life challenges. Because your wife has "always" evinced this lack of interest, I doubt that taking hormones postmenopause will magically dispel a lifelong pattern.

You asked about normalcy. That's a culturally defined term. What's normal in Kathmandu may be considered outrageous in Indianapolis. Because we are a society that thinks of sexual interaction as mutual and reciprocal, however, it is not normal (to answer your first question) for one partner to feel such antipathy toward the other partner's passion—and for such a long time. I don't hear empathy on your wife's part: "What must this be like for you?" Nor do I hear any self-observation: "I wonder why it is that I am not only uninterested in sex, but feel compelled to put you down for your interest in it?" Granted, I am hearing only your side, but something's rotten in the state of your marriage—and you've got to get to the heart of it.

Sex therapists approach problems from the perspectives of personal distress and interpersonal problems. By your account, your wife doesn't seem personally troubled by her lack of interest, but she does have big interpersonal problems with you about sex. You, on the other hand, are experiencing both personal distress and interpersonal problems. A sex therapist (to answer your second question) will be helpful to both of you in resolving this couples sexual problem.

You can find a sex therapist who is credentialed through the American Association of Sex Educators, Counselors, and Therapists at www.aasect.org. If your wife is unwilling to see a specialist in sexual problems, go to a general couples therapist instead.

Invite your wife to participate in counseling with the goal of improving your relationship, not fixing her. You may find that intimacy and communication—the building blocks of any strong relationship—have eroded through simple inattention. Rebuilding that foundation should be the first step toward putting your house back in order.

**Q** I've been in a committed relationship with the same man for the past 17 years. While my libido goes down the drain, he is happily enjoying the effects of Viagra and Levitra.

He wants me to climax first so he can get aroused, at which point the meds can take over and he can have a better climax; meanwhile he tries to stimulate me, but it is harder and harder for me to become even remotely excited.

I changed my blood-pressure medication to a product clinically proven *not* to interfere with orgasms, but I am only occasionally aroused enough to "really" participate. I can climax with masturbation, and sometimes it is really nice, but I still do not have a libido worth anything.

Where can women turn to stimulate our libido? When we were still "in lust," I smoked marijuana to enjoy the sexual relationship, but as time went by I gave that up. In the interim, nothing better has come along. Do you have any words of wisdom for me?

**A** While your partner enjoys a first-class ride into aging with his tray table in the fully upright and locked position, you are back in coach, pawing through the seat pocket in front of you for the proper blood-pressure pills. Not exactly the futuristic flight of fancy you'd planned, is it?

Some people enjoy robust libidos well into their 80s. Others notice diminutions at half that age. However, you are correct in believing that the libido—however frail—can be resuscitated.

But since I'm the expert and you seek my wisdom, let me tell you what's wrong with your current relationship:

First, you and your partner are overly focused on outside sources to generate your sexual responses. You once used pot to get it on; now he wants to use you in much the same way.

Second, you are both obsessed with results; nothing shuts

down arousal faster than a "performance" mind-set. So forget about orgasms, and just enjoy the moment.

A love life where he gets all the fun and you get all the frustration is a lopsided (not to mention stone-cold) bummer. Be honest with your partner about your desire to rebalance things. For starters, experiment with sex play that isn't quite so patterned and rigid. Instead of focusing on orgasm, spend an entire bedtime reading sexy stories to each other. Or try a sensual massage, with private parts decreed "off limits" for the duration of the event. Your interest will be sparked by staying focused in the present.

If orgasms remain on your must-have list, continue to practice through masturbation. Learn how to move them from "nice" to "much nicer."

Unlike so many other aspects of modern life, the management of your libido cannot be outsourced; you cannot delegate it to a pill or to your partner. Attend to your own sensory pleasure and you'll wind up enhancing your sexual experience. The best way to turn on, you may find, is to regularly tune in to yourself.

**Q** My wife may be starting menopause. She has no desire for sex of any type. Is this nonsexual phase a normal part of menopause?

**A** No... yes... and all of the above.

*No.* Perimenopause—the time leading up to menopause, beginning in the late 30s for most women—is a normal part of a woman's journey through midlife. For the majority of women, neither perimenopause nor menopause itself suppresses sexual desire or arousal. Although a woman in her 60s possesses only about half the testosterone of a woman in her 20s, women often report an increase in their sexual responsivity at this time of their lives. Many women identify this heightened sensitivity as stemming from their overall sense of greater personal freedom and enjoyment.

*Yes.* It can affect sexual desire. Declining levels of estrogen and testosterone trigger perimenopause. In some women, these lower thresholds negatively affect mood; they also diminish energy, sexual desire, and sexual response.

*All of the above.* Menopause can serve as a turning point. Midlife centers around raising children (often those troublesome teens), worrying about work, and caring for parents and other older relatives. These factors are practically a prescription for decreased sexual desire, which is known to result from stress and busy schedules. Now stretch these role demands over a decade or more, add in the fact that a couple's longtime relationship may have come to lack luster, and you get some women deciding that "menopause" means "me no pause for sex anymore"!

If your wife's lethargic libida bothers her, she should talk with her doctor. For some women, a time-limited hormone therapy or other medications can help. As research continues in this area, it will expand the options available.

I can anticipate your next question, so allow me to answer it: The best way to turn a "No" into a "Yes" is to be supportive and well informed about everything spelled out above (and more). Above all, demonstrate a genuine concern for what engenders her lack of desire. You both stand to benefit (or you can lie down, if that's more comfortable) when it rebounds!

**Q** My wife of less than a year has a hang-up about being nude in front of anyone, including me. It's very frustrating, especially when we are going to make love. I have seen her by accident and she is beautiful. Yet she always insists that the room be completely dark. How can I cure her of this?

**A** You're not alone in your frustration; many women struggle with negative body images or are uncomfortable with nudity. Brown University psychiatry professor Katharine Phillips, M.D., characterizes this as "disabling anxiety" about their bodies. "Some people may even have a genetic vulnerability to these feelings," she adds.

A number of strategies may be of help—to both of you. Remember, this is a touchy topic for your wife; it's therefore highly likely that it will be tough for her to talk about it. That in turn means there must not be the merest hint of condemnation in anything you say regarding her requests. You used the words "hang-up" and "cure" in your question; bag those, because nobody is sick here. At all costs, avoid inflammatory adjectives ("uptight," "prudish") when you discuss this difference between the two of you.

Next, ponder the positives. You and your bride are regularly making love, and you find her beautiful. Make sure that you are affirming about her looks and your love life. And because your wife's body radar is so finely tuned, refrain from wisecracks about anyone else's body type.

My instinct tells me that a little homegrown cognitive behavioral therapy may be in order for you.

For the cognitive, choose a time that is relaxed and not sexual, and ask your wife if the two of you can talk about this difference you have. Explain that for you there would be increased intimacy in visually looking at each other's bodies. Ask if she can explain what exactly makes her uncomfortable: Is it that she does not like to be looked at, or that she's embarrassed about a specific body part? Listen respectfully. Do not try to correct her view of herself or her social learning. Acknowledge that you see it differently, and that you'd like to keep the dialogue going. If she gets defensive or angry, remind her that you "come in peace" and are simply trying to build a positive and more intimate relationship. At the same time, don't let her off the hook. Explain that this difference between you is significant enough that you want to keep working to resolve it.

Now for the behavioral therapy. Your wife may find it easier to be less than fully clothed in a nonsexual but playful setting. You can walk the beach in your bathing suits, try water aerobics, or take a class in massage. Remove the spotlight from her and shine it instead on your shared adventure. Interestingly, some women find it easier to be in their bodies if they learn some new body moves: yoga, tap dancing, or—for one woman I knew—belly dancing.

Another behavioral tip: Ask if the two of you can cuddle while wearing underwear. Or could you make love by the dawn's early light? Try to ease her toward being more comfortable with nudity.

My advice can take you only so far. If your wife resists all efforts to change, consider going to sex therapy together. Some who suffer great anxiety about their bodies have found relief through counseling and certain medications available by prescription. If you go the medication route, consult with a physician about antianxiety drugs. "Medications can help people obsess less about what they see as their imperfections," says Dr. Phillips.

So... begin slowly, focus on your shared experience, and the two of you should be able to migrate toward the light. You've got a lot going for you.

**Q** My husband wants me to talk dirty to him. I've never said bad words—not even "S**t!" when I'm mad. Is there a book I can learn from? He thinks it may help our sex life.

**A** If you've ever purchased anything from a garage sale, you know that one person's trash is another person's treasure. And so it is with couples; talking dirty is offal for some, awesome for others.

I must admit I'm impressed by your commitment to try something different. Because you both sound interested in jump-starting your sex life—albeit with some initial hesitation or awkwardness—you might just find that lots of bad words aren't so bad after all. So if you decide to stretch your imaginations, yes, there is a book you can learn from: It's by a sex therapist named Lonnie Barbach, and it's titled *Turnons: Pleasing Yourself While You Please Your Lover.* As a how-to guide for improving your sex life, I recommend it highly. (See especially Barbach's take on "Aural Sex"—get it?—on page 7.)

Many a couple finds sexual playacting to be a fun, enjoyable, and mutually pleasurable pursuit. You can pretend to be an actress playing a part. The two of you can plan in advance how the scene might unfold. Sometimes it helps to have something you can do—such as give a massage—while you're saying the words. You can venture into this a little at

a time: Try it for 30 seconds, perhaps, then revert to something you feel more comfortable doing.

If talking dirty leaves a bad taste in your mouth, don't
stress; plenty of other innovations can spice up your sex
life. Complex creatures that we are, we like our bedtime
routines, but dislike routine in our bed times.

# The ABCs Of Pleasure

**Q** After being divorced for 10 years, I'm in a relationship again. During foreplay I have no problem attaining a strong erection, but then, to our mutual frustration, I sometimes go soft just as we begin making love. She is kind about this, but it gives me doubts that I fear may worsen the problem. Any suggestions?

**A** It's a real psychological turn-on for a woman when her partner can be so honest about a sexual concern. I like your style.

Erectile quality can change over time, so you'd be wise to check the systems. Visit a urologist to see if there's a medical problem. Ask if medications might help. They're not panaceas, but they are helpful to many.

Before your next play date, consider experimenting with some self-stimulation to figure out how best to maintain your erection and arousal. You might find that certain positions and stimulations are best. Tell your partner what works. However sizzling your connection, she's not a mind reader, and she will be delighted to know. (If this makes you nervous, rehearse beforehand what you'd like to tell her.) Also, if you've been given medication, use it first by yourself to learn how it works.

Out-of-bed activities can influence your performance, too. Save heavy meals or drinking alcohol for after sex. If your health permits, make your prelude to foreplay a little exercise to get your blood flowing, such as climbing the stairs twice or taking a hot shower.

When making love, avoid lying flat on your back—that can inhibit blood flow—and encourage your partner to stimulate such "erectile zones" as your lips, earlobes, nipples, and perineum (the sensitive area behind the scrotum). Keep your mind focused on her; if you start to drift toward anxiety, say "Stop!" (in your head, not out loud) and repeat a positive thought. Something like, "We're turned on and this feels great!"

**Q** **I'm dating a wonderful woman who enjoys sex, but she's had a hysterectomy and takes a long time to climax, if at all. I tend to climax before she does, so I have trouble fully pleasing her. What can help?**

## ·····Sexual Health·······················
# FOR WOMEN

**W**hen it comes to sex, negative messages begin in the delivery room and roll right into menopause:

"It's not about you, it's about him."

"If you're a mom, you're too busy for sex."

"After menopause, you're too old for sex."

Whether you've ignored these messages or felt their burden, a few late-breaking facts of life can dynamically improve a woman's sexual health after 40. After that, the pleasure is all yours.

*Don't wait—lubricate!* Had uncomfortable burning or pain? Felt like saying, "Not tonight, honey—having sex feels like exfoliation"? Thinning of the vaginal walls and a natural decrease in lubrication with age can cause this sensation. Try a vaginal cream (Estrace), suppository (Vagifem), or cervical ring (Estring). Considered safe by health-care providers, each emits small amounts of estrogen just to the vagina—greatly improving wetness, tissue health, and comfort. (Lubrin and Replens are non-estrogen alternatives.)

*Ditch that seven-year itch.* For extra slip and slide during sex, find a lubricant that's not sticky or itchy. There are many to choose from—available at drug stores or at www.drugstore.com. For a really smooth ride, look for glycerin-free lubes or try pure vitamin E oil, olive oil, or egg whites (no, they needn't be whipped).

*Help your "innie" out.* Boys have outies; girls have innies. Yours needs regular stretching, by intercourse or a dilator. If you're having regular intercourse, you're already stretching your vagina. If you're unattached and uninterested, skip stretching. But know that life is unpredictable; many of my patients concluded they'd never have sex again, only to then meet the partner of their dreams.

*Kegel.* Contract and relax the muscles of your pelvic floor daily. The improved muscle tone will do wonders for your orgasms.

*Get (and keep) attitude.* Women have sexual fantasies throughout their lives, and can remain orgasmic well into their 90s. —SALLIE FOLEY

**A** Arousal and orgasm are among the great mysteries of life. Some of us are tortoises. Some of us are hares. It's hard to say if your partner's hysterectomy is really a factor. "Any pelvic surgery has the potential to damage the nerves and blood vessels, but the research on whether hysterectomy hurts or helps a woman's sexual function is mixed," says Aline P. Zoldbrod, Ph.D., a Boston-based sex therapist.

You two need to have a candid talk about lovemaking. Ask her which part of sex she likes most—and least. Most important, ask how you could arouse her more before sex. "Ask if she ever gives herself an orgasm and, if so, what kinds of stimulation work best for her," Zoldbrod says. Her answers may reveal that her hysterectomy isn't the culprit.

Stop focusing so much on timing. I suppose simultaneous orgasm has happened somewhere in the world, but trying to synchronize your liftoffs isn't helpful. There are about 3,000 ways to please her after you've climaxed, and she can walk you through most of them.

Also, don't assume that she feels cheated until you've asked her. From your note, it doesn't seem as if she's complaining. "Many women enjoy the closeness and warmth of sex, even if they don't climax," Zoldbrod says. But if she is bothered by this and nothing helps, she may want to talk to her doctor. Low arousal can often be medically treated.

**Q** When did Aline Zoldbrod make the above statement about women enjoying sex even if they don't climax—in the year 1900? That remark is right out of the patriarchal double standard that women have been striving to shed for the last 40 years. In the 21st century, most of us expect to enjoy an orgasm at *least* as many times as our partners.

A If there's a double standard for orgasm, nature landed women on the lucky side. Women enjoy orgasm throughout their lives—well into their 90s. Nor do women require a refractory period, as men do; that is, they have no physiological need for a rest period between orgasms. So congratulations on landing in the right body—and enjoy those orgasms at any time! In fact, you should be able to have orgasms *more often* than your male partner.

Why, then, would Aline Zoldbrod—a respected sex therapist whose publicly acclaimed work includes *Sex Smart: How Your Childhood Shaped Your Sexual Life and What to Do About It*—be correct? For years, patriarchy was indeed the rule. Women's sexuality was ignored or downright abused. Lacking the "right genitalia," women supposedly couldn't enjoy sex at all.

Nowadays, of course, sexologists no longer box in sexual experience. Consider this manifesto: The skin is a sexual organ, the brain is an organ of pleasure, and you can refuse to be pigeonholed or bullied into "having" to have anything, whether it's oral sex, intercourse, or orgasm.

Each person or couple should define for themselves what constitutes "pleasurable sex." That elusive but satisfying goal is highly contextual, personal, and amazing—in all its myriad forms.

Q My husband and I have been married eight years. We're very much in love. The problem is that making love can never be spontaneous. It has to be planned, since he needs help from medication that he can administer only according to certain rules his doctor gave us: three hours after meals, not late at night, and so on. (He can't take any of the newer pills.)

**What measures can we take to make our love life feel more spontaneous?**

**A** I'm going to assume you've discussed all possibilities with your doctor regarding a change in medication. I'm also going to assume that if your husband's problem isn't wholly due to a physical condition, you've explored another consideration: Many men don't lose the ability to get or sustain an erection; they just require more sexual stimulation than they did when they were younger. Sometimes ratcheting up the excitement level can help a man operate without pharmaceutical assistance.

If those options don't apply, remember that the only thing the two of you can't do at the drop of a skirt is to have intercourse. Every other sexual option remains available to you, at any time. (Please don't make me itemize them all.)

"Too many of us have a limited, intercourse-centric view of lovemaking," says psychologist Joel Block, the author of *Sex Over 50*. "Caressing, holding, and being playful without the pressure of performance can be wonderful." You can have spontaneous foreplay—even if it's just cuddling in bed while eating low-fat ice cream—while you're waiting for the blessings of modern pharmacology to manifest themselves.

Further, there is no reason why the anticipation of a regular Friday night hookup cannot be as exciting as an out-of-the-blue quickie.

**Q** My husband and I have been married for 33 years. We have a decent sex life, but as soon as it begins for him, it's over. The foreplay is great; after that, however, the session becomes disappointing for me. Any advice?

**A** Reading between the lines, it sounds like your husband is experiencing premature ejaculation (PE). This most common form of male sexual problem can have psychological, physical, or environmental causes. It is difficult to define, except to say that the man experiences orgasm before he wants to.

PE can throw a relationship into a "negative feedback loop." That is to say, men often withdraw from sustained sexual involvement because they feel ashamed that they orgasm too quickly. This in turn can lead the man's partner to feel frustrated, angry, or hopeless. Even if a partner pretends things are fine, the man detects the disappointment, feels more shame, and withdraws further still. Thus does the cycle reinforce itself.

PE can range from the simple—a lack of understanding of ejaculatory control, for example—to the complicated, such as the dovetailing of a man's sex-negative upbringing with high amounts of physiological anxiety. The reaction of the other partner in the sexual relationship varies widely, too. Those who see themselves as members of the same team as their partner tend to be accepting of PE; others focus on the problem rather than the person and elect to interpret every instance of PE as further corroboration that their sex life is lousy.

Thirty-three years won't change in 33 days. Begin with a self-assessment of your own teamwork ability. Can you be encouraging, kind, and well-informed? I suggest you educate yourself about PE by viewing the DVD *You Can Last Longer*

by Derek Polonsky, M.D. (available at www.bettersex.com).
You may also want to read *Coping with Premature Ejaculation: How to Overcome PE, Please Your Partner, and Have Great Sex* by Michael Metz and Barry McCarthy.

Next, talk with your husband about your concerns. Creating a happier sex life will require patience. Isn't it ironic that our culture celebrates the sexual liberation of a woman who is able to climax quickly but stigmatizes a man who possesses the same ability?

**Q** I can get an erection easily; my problem is ejaculation—an enjoyable but increasingly rare event when I have sex. Can you help?

**A** Gee, I don't know—where do you live?

But seriously... Let's see if we can't heat things up enough to move you from "rare" to "well done"! We'll focus on function, fiction, and friction.

*Function:* Be rested. Skip alcohol and heavy meals. Take a hot shower to get that all-important blood flowing through your arteries and veins.

*Fiction:* Concentrate on arousal. Good sex starts between your ears, not between your legs. Make sure you're tuned in. Focus on your partner—or, if you're flying solo, tune in to a great fantasy—and let yourself be carried away. (Note: It helps to keep those fantasies simmering on a back burner between sexual activities; just don't get sidetracked—or run off the road—by your daydreams!)

*Friction:* Heighten skin sensation by tightening your thigh muscles during sex and using a firmer touch to get aroused. As we get older, arousal is dependent on a stronger

····Sexual Health········································
## FOR MEN

**M**en want sex that makes them feel great about the quality of the experience they're sharing with their partner. As a result, EQ, or erectile quality, has become the most up-to-date way to describe the caliber of a man's sexual experience. In my practice, however, I've heard men express dissatisfaction with their sex lives even when taking Viagra or a similar drug. For a rise in your own EQ, try these nonpharmaceutical ways to tune in and turn on:

*Outside the bedroom:*

Heavy meals and extra pounds stymie arousal. As for alcohol, Shakespeare said it best: "Drink decreaseth performance."

Research shows a direct correlation between exercise and increased sexual satisfaction—so get up, get out, and move that body. You'll also decrease stress and boost your energy and mood.

Sleep: Seven to eight hours a night, please. This natural antidepressant lets your neurochemistry function at its best.

Testosterone: It doesn't take much of the stuff to drive libido, but it does take some. Stop at the doctor's for a general health check.

Practice kegeling—the exercise in which you tense and then release the muscles in the pelvic floor. These exercises tone up the PC muscle, facilitating more pleasurable orgasms.

Herbal remedies have mixed results. Before you try them, go to a reputable health food store and talk to knowledgeable personnel.

*In the bedroom (preferably with a partner):*

The goal: Limit distractions and increase erotic focus. Be at your best—romantic and happy. Light candles; have a great lube handy.

Talk during sex. After all, you're sharing this moment with her.

Change positions. Doing it the "same old way" causes your mind to wander and prevents sexual tension from building. (That's a bad thing.)

Focus on your partner's arousal and response. Women like a lover with a slow hand and a steady touch.  —SALLIE FOLEY nervous-system response, which is necessary for triggering orgasm. Consider purchasing a vibrator to use on your own body for additional stimulation. Yep, they're for guys too. That deep vibratory stimulation will wake up sleepy nerve endings and send a stronger message to your brain.

You can use a vibrator intended for body massage, find one at a sex-toy store, or go online to the reputable good-vibes.com (no pop-ups or cookies on your computer). Firm stroking of your perineum (the skin between the scrotum and anus) will stimulate the prostate, increasing sexual sensation. Remember that your refractory (or recovery) period grows longer as you age, so give your body a day off here and there.

And finally, a prediction: Keep experimenting and asking questions. The more you learn about your response, the better you'll get at achieving climax.

# Making Love Last

**Q** Our last son just left for college, and it's created a weird stillness between my husband and me. How can we reconnect?

**A** Your son took more than your sound system—he took a lot of human energy, too. He may have been the strongest link between you and your husband. Often, in the tumult of raising and caring for children, parents lose touch with each other (hamster-wrangling isn't what lit Bogey and Bergman's fire). Now, each of you has to bring more wattage into the house to replace the boy's.

Courting each other again can lead to an inspiring second wind of affection. Perform small acts of consideration. If your husband likes Oreos, buy them for him. Don't be afraid to be corny and sweet. Most important, talk over the need to reconnect, even if this seems odd because you've been together for so long.

If the thought of discussing this makes you cringe, be aware that empty-nest stillness isn't always caused by having nothing to talk about. Sometimes, it's the opposite. "Many couples, while raising kids, have an unspoken agreement not to talk about painful issues that they fear might blow their marriage apart," says Atlanta sex therapist Jeanne Shaw, Ph.D. The partners may remain afraid of cracking the seal even after the kids leave. "Once couples decide that they're staying together for life, however, they often feel safe to defuse these issues," says Shaw. Without fear of abandonment, they set to work on thinking, together and separately, about what's right and wrong with the marriage. Often, notes Shaw, this freedom "can lead to more authentic relationships, even more intense sexual lives."

Don't hesitate to see a therapist. That "weird stillness" may be a bigger threat to your marriage than the dark corners you're afraid to explore.

**Q** Is it normal for my husband of 35-plus years suddenly to want me to wear racy lingerie, garter belts, and stockings? The sex is great, but I wonder if this happens to other couples.

**A** If two grown people enjoy something, who cares if it's "normal"? But note the word two. "Sex play has to be

entered into freely, and both partners need the option to
say no," says Jean Koehler, past president of the American
Association of Sex Educators, Counselors, and Therapists.
If the come-and-get-me undies are out of your comfort
zone, don't feel compelled to strut around for him like Sally
Bowles from *Cabaret*.

But to quote you, "The sex is great." Hmmm... not something you hear every day from a woman who's been married
35 years. Before you nix the naughty knickers, try on these
thoughts:

First, high-caliber women do wear sexy lingerie. Character and style make you a lady, not all-cotton granny panties.

Second, your husband's lingerie lust will ring a bell with
many men, who require more mojo to get ready for romance
as they age. Crimson-laced thigh-highs can be visual
Viagra. Don't think this means he's bored with you; it may
be the opposite. You two have been together since Wood-
stock, but you still make him feel like a bong-crazy teen.
Relationships often benefit from newness, Koehler adds,
"if both partners are open to it."

My survey of friends suggests that lots of women face
a Victoria's Secret moment. So try this compromise: Shop
together for lingerie that's subtle enough for you but slinky
enough for him.

**Q** My wife and I don't sleep as soundly as we used to, and
I'd prefer to start sleeping in a separate bed. She thinks this
will hurt our marriage. Is there any truth to that?

**A** Sleeping with your wife is worth fighting for, so don't
go gently into separate beds. Try everything reasonable to

keep cuddling compatibly. If snoring is a culprit, it's often curable. So get an evaluation at the nearest disorders clinic of a major medical center. In addition, check out the terrific resource entitled *Good Nights* by Gary K. Zammit, M.D., and Jane A. Zanca.

You can also try one of those dualzone mattresses—or pushing twin beds together—so that she can wrestle her demons without disturbing you.

But if you have explored everything else and just can't share the sheets serenely, separate beds is a good idea. Low-quality sleep puts both of you at greater risk for lots of health problems—everything from bone loss to car accidents. It can also lead to arguments.

Well-rested people are just better partners. Be sure to talk the bed-divorce through with your wife; make it clear that you love sleeping with her, but that restorative sleep is important for both of you.

"Your marriage won't suffer as long as you're both determined to maintain intimacy," according to Linda Newhart Lotz, Ph.D., a psychologist and sex therapist in Gainesville, Florida. "Since the only problem is the actual sleeping, spend some time together in one bed before going your separate sleeping ways."

After a few minutes of reading or chatting, or sex, just slip away to your separate nests—either right after she nods off, or just before you do. If you set your alarm for five minutes before hers, you can even slither back in next to Juliet right before she wakes. Also, try to compensate for any touching shortfall by upping the allotment of midday hugs, affectionate pats, and cozy moments on the couch.

## ..... The Secrets of .....................................
# LONG-LASTING MARRIAGE

**A**ll married couples should learn the art of battle as they should learn the art of making love." Sun Tzu? Nope—Ann Landers. Asked to define successful marriage, the columnist elaborated, "Good battle is objective and honest—never vicious or cruel. Good battle is healthy and constructive, and brings to a marriage the principle of equal partnership." Fair fighting—plus open communication and mutual respect—are key ingredients in a long, healthy marriage. But what else does it take to keep a union going strong 30, 40, even 50 or more years? Brown University psychiatry professor Scott Haltzman, M.D., says it all depends on how the marriage unfolds over time: "How a couple deals with the natural evolution of marriage defines the difference between those couples who are happily married for decades and those who don't make it past one presidential campaign."

Many couples see themselves as yin to the other's yang. In 62 years of marriage, for example, Carl and Estelle Reiner have shared a lifetime of laughter and "balancing each other." Carl, creator of *The Dick Van Dyke Show*, finds comfort in his wife's quiet wisdom; Estelle clearly adores his dry wit. "We used to hold hands because we wanted to," says Carl. "Now we hold hands so we don't fall."

"It's a give-and-take affair," says Joel Mcleod of his 64-year marriage to Eva. "Don't think you'll issue all the instructions."

Jim and Jeanne O'Donnell have been married 53 years. When they sit beside each other, they look like a couple of school kids in the first stages of young love. But their marriage hit its share of rough patches—notably Jim's bout with alcoholism. "Those were difficult times," Jeanne reflects today. "I definitely gave some thought to leaving." Patience and tolerance saw them through: "Without the loyalty and affection," notes Jim, "the marriage could never have survived." —SACHA COHEN

**Q** My husband retired a few years ago, but I'm still working full-time at a job I enjoy. He's unhappy about our different lifestyles, and I feel like I have to choose between my job and him. Any advice?

**A** Your big mistake was not talking through your retirement plans while he was working. Many couples, assuming retirement will be easy, underestimate the problems that can occur. "The sudden freedom from work can unleash feelings that the nine-to-five routine kept in check," says Sally Kope, M.S.W., coauthor of *Sex Matters for Women*.

Ask your husband exactly what's bothering him about your working. This might be sensitive. If he's old school, he may feel embarrassed that you're earning a paycheck while he's still sporting his pajamas in the middle of the morning. Lots of men see breadwinning as a male duty. He may think you're working because you worry about your financial future, which he could read as an indictment of his own earning power. To defuse this, make it clear that you're working because you enjoy your job.

Of course, maybe he just has trouble filling his day. Unless your job consumes your every waking hour—including nights and weekends—you're entitled to do it without his sulking. Isolation and boredom are his problems to fix. If you need to help, buy him a new bicycle with the cash you're raking in.

Finally, if you're comfortable doing it, agree on a date when you will retire—and what you'll do together afterward. Having a plan often makes partners feel more in synch with each other.

**Q** My wife and I have both put on about 50 pounds since we got married, and it's starting to affect our marriage. She can no longer walk long distances, and our lovemaking would be much better if we lost weight. My wife doesn't support me when I suggest we join Weight Watchers or start eating differently. How can I persuade her to change with me?

**A** Get inside her head for 10 seconds. Weight gain strikes at the heart of self-esteem. This is particularly true for women, given our cruel worship of the hourglass figure. Your wife may feel your suggestions about weight loss mean you're no longer attracted to her—and that means your first mission is to make sure she knows you are, even if you aren't. Remember the single smartest thing that anyone ever noted: People rarely change unless they feel accepted as they are.

Your health is at risk, so using the guilt approach isn't out of bounds. Try some variation of "I can't imagine life without you. I want us to be healthy together." If you have children or grandchildren, underscore how much she matters to them. Emphasize how precious she is, rather than how heavy she is. Precious things should be cared for.

If your wife refuses to exercise, bear in mind that the initial resistance is often the biggest hurdle. Many people get quickly enthused about how much better even a modicum of physical activity makes them feel. Try the old marital barter strategy to get her started: If she will walk with you for half an hour after dinner every night, you will stop ordering those "Carb Lover" pizzas while watching college football on TV.

Let's say you've employed all these stratagems and your

wife still simply refuses to join you in losing weight—then what? Forge ahead without her. "You can't allow her reluctance to prevent you from taking responsibility for your own health," says Jeanne Shaw, Ph.D., a clinical psychologist who counsels couples. Join Weight Watchers on your own. Start cooking healthier meals. When you start shedding the pounds, chances are good your wife will get on board as well. Every compliment you get will motivate her—and you'll get plenty.

One motivational trick for both of you: Don't think about all the pounds you have to lose. Instead, consider that if you lose just one ounce per day, there will be 22.8 pounds less of you at this time next year.

# Life Is Messy

*If we had no faults of our own,*
*we should not take half so much satisfaction*
*in observing those of other people.*
—FRANÇOIS, DUC DE LA ROCHEFOUCAULD

# Life Is Messy

TAKE ANY COUPLE—no, take the happiest couple you know. Scratch the surface of their partnership and you'll find they've had their struggles. Talk to your friends—those with and without partners—and you'll discover every one of them has a story to tell. For when it comes to relationships, if a human can imagine it, somewhere a human has done it—or suffered its consequences. From the boorish to the bizarre, people place themselves in some peculiar pickles (and vice versa)—and they may or may not be actively seeking an exit strategy from their personal predicament.

If you're in a relationship, some bond other than the mortgage makes you stick together. You get to pick the glue, but in my work as a marital and sex therapist I've found that most people choose friendship, love, and commitment to shared goals and values.

If you've encountered problems in your relationship—if, that is, you're a human and you're alive—you must accept the fact that no matter what happens next, you will be in pain. If it's the pain of staying in the problem, the ache will be a familiar one that changes nothing. If it's the pain of repairing the problem, get ready for some new pangs that can move you out of the mess.

Adults seeking professional help for a quandary of their own creation tend to describe the situation thus: "I can't fix this problem, but you can, and therefore you should—just don't tell me what to do. Get me out of this pain—but not necessarily out of this relationship. I've suffered enough, so don't make me feel any worse."

Whenever I encounter a description such as this, I try to remind myself what I've learned in 20 years of clinical practice, to say nothing of a three-year detour through divinity school: Some people want to complain, and others want to change. (A third group wants to change, but needs to complain for a long time before they engage the clutch.)

Which group feels right for you?

Read on if you're ready for change, for in this section you'll discover how others have negotiated (or not) the hazards that pockmark Relationship Road—and how they're moving ahead in life. You'll find sidebars along the way on modeling mature sexuality for teenagers, the secrets of durable unions, and a sexual pioneer who started us down this path in the first place.

## 7

# Bumps in the Road

**Q** I recently discovered that my husband has been pulling up porn on the Internet. We've been married for 25 years, and this is the first time I've seen him do anything like this. I assure you, he is not neglected in any way regarding sex with me. Should I be concerned?

**A** Although the world might be better off with less simulated sex everywhere, levelheaded adults should be able to enjoy erotic pictures in private without undermining their relationships, their immortal souls, or the republic.

So your husband's interest in salacious words or pictures probably does not mean he has lost interest in you or your sex life together. "People often have sexual fantasies that do not bear on whether or not they're in love with their partners or capable of getting aroused by them," says Michael Bader, author of *Arousal: The Secret Logic of Sexual Fantasies*. Scanning some blue photos or videos might be a harmless way of dealing with a bit of restlessness—natural in a long marriage.

Now, back to how your husband isn't neglected "in any way" when it comes to sex. You're a willing and energetic partner, but your husband may feel nervous about asking you to slake some of his secret thirsts.

His porn peek has given you an opportunity to help him air these desires, and that could benefit you both. Bader suggests mentioning to him that you noticed he was surfing through some spicy stuff online. Just be careful to present it in a strictly nonjudgmental way. Reassure him that you don't think he's doing a bad thing, or that you're living with the devil. If you two can begin talking about it, you could get him to open up about what he likes to see online and how he's feeling about your sex life. That conversation could lead to a lot more fun for both of you.

**Q** After 30 years of marriage, things have started coming to light that persuade me my husband has lied to me all along about his past. He refuses to divulge things such as his prior military service status, even though we are reaching the age where we would qualify for tax advantages.

He feels that his past belongs to him alone, and that I should be willing to let it go at that. I feel that I've been manipulated—my trust has been violated—and that counseling, separation, or divorce is in order.

What do you think?

**A** More than 30 years ago, your husband had an experience that he has never fully discussed with you. Because his past has been there all along, however, it will be difficult to sort out at this late date whether this was a case of deliberate deceit on his part or whether it has more to do with painful or shameful experiences he simply doesn't want anyone else—even his wife—to know about.

Why has this become a potential marital ties-breaker only now? Is it really a question of mere tax advantages? Or is it a more profound exploration of your overall emotional security? Perhaps you are asking yourself, "If he won't come clean on this issue, what others don't I know about?"

You are wise to suggest marital counseling as one possible solution. Your husband may not want to discuss the past, but in order to have a future, you both need to reach an accommodation in the present. I encourage the two of you to work together with a therapist to find a pathway back to the common ground and experiences you shared for three decades. If he refuses to walk that road with you, you'll have to seriously consider the second or third solutions you outlined at the end of your question.

**Q** I've been seeing a man for four years. Although his wife died seven years ago, he still wears his wedding ring. This makes me uncomfortable. I don't know how to approach him about it. Also, how do we introduce each other? I've been saying "my friend," but he's more than that.

**A** His band of gold is his form of self-defense. "Sometimes partners hold on to previous spouses to avoid the feelings of grief that come with a deep letting-go," says couples therapist Doug Moseley of Taos, New Mexico. Wearing his wedding ring might smooth the ragged edge off his loss, but it may also keep him from giving you his whole heart. "If you want more, you'll have to express your feelings," says Moseley, author—with his wife, Naomi—of *Making Your Second Marriage a First-Class Success*. "But be prepared to discover that he would rather hold on to the ring than make a full commitment to you."

The trick here is to present your feelings without indicting him and to show that you honor his memories of his dearly departed. Try this: "I respect your loss, but it makes me feel like I'm second in your heart." If he cares for you, he'll probably put your feelings ahead of his dependence on his wife. If he doesn't, you two need to have a more serious talk.

As for introductions, "friend" doesn't reveal the depth of your connection. Some people say "lover," but that's just plain wrong. We don't need *Kama Sutra* images at the dinner party. It's not perfect, but for unmarried couples I prefer the old-fashioned "sweetheart." Sure, it's corny—but couldn't the world use a little more hard-core corn?

**Q** What's up with men who refuse to say those three little words but are quick to describe it with four little letters?

When a relationship is intimate, it shouldn't be hard to say, "I love you." (In fact, it should be hard *not* to say it.) But it makes him flinch when he hears that simple statement. What's with him, anyway?

## The Man Who
# INVENTED SEX

Biology professor Alfred Kinsey was teaching a course on marriage at Indiana University in the late 1930s when he began interviewing people of all ages about their sexual practices. The sessions led to two landmark works, *Sexual Behavior in the Human Male* (1948) and *Sexual Behavior in the Human Female* (1953), which threw open the nation's bedroom doors to curious onlookers. Researcher Edward Laumann says Kinsey's interview techniques revolutionized the field: "He asked, 'How often do you masturbate?' with the assumption that everyone does it. He normalized the conversation." Kinsey's research revealed that 90 percent of males and 62 percent of females masturbate regularly. They also indicated 40 percent of men and 25 percent of women engaging in extramarital sex.

Kinsey plumbed the sexual habits of older Americans too. "The steady decline in the incidences and frequencies of marital coitus," he intoned in *Sexual Behavior in the Human Female*, "must be the product of aging processes in the male. There is little evidence of any aging in the sexual capacities of the female until late in her life."

Insisting that most bedroom dysfunction stems from cultural repression, Kinsey strove to dispel the notion of "normal" sexuality. As the 2004 movie *Kinsey* made clear, that became his personal crusade as well. Though married to the same woman for 35 years, the man who had been raised in a strict Methodist household energetically sampled both masochism and homosexuality.

Kinsey was attacked in the early 1950s for allegedly encouraging communism. In 1954, the Rockefeller Foundation funding that had sustained his research for 13 years—and helped establish the famed Institute for Sex Research—was abruptly withdrawn. Soon after, the 62-year-old Kinsey died of heart disease. If he did not unleash the sexual revolution himself, Kinsey at least taught Americans to discuss previously taboo subjects without shame. —CHRISTINA IANZITO

**A** I put this question to my psychologist husband, and I think I'm starting to see what you mean: He thinks those three little words are "Let's have sex!"

But seriously, who knows what's up with your man? (As you can see, I have enough trouble with my own). Perhaps he's ambivalent about the relationship—psychologese for saying he may not be certain he loves you. Or maybe he's just a little twitchy (the clinical term is "emotionally distant") and can't help cowering when you verbally cuddle up.

Test-drive this behavior-modification program:

Begin each day by facing each other. Breathe in deeply. Breathe out deeply. Look him straight in the eye.

*You say:* "Repeat after me." *[Then sigh loudly]*

*He says:* "Repeat after me." *[Remind him to sigh loudly.]*

*You:* "I love you." *[Loud sigh]*

*Him:* "Geez, gimme a frickin' break here, wouldja?!" *[Loud, spontaneous sigh]*

*You:* "Excellent! You've mastered the sigh—now all we have to work on is the words."

If your wordless wooer is dreamy in every other way, consider overlooking his tongue-tied temperament. Tell him you're disappointed, but that you'll make an exception for symbolic language… just so long as all the other symbolic gestures are in place.

If, however, you find that his deficiency extends to more than three little words, consider moving on and creating a new life without him. Most lovers use language as a tool for connecting with each other. Someone who deprives you of this may have a toolbox too empty to build a nest for two.

**Q** My husband is a breast man, and I don't have any. I am not even a 32A. My breasts are like those of a six-year-old—there's no "them" there.

For the life of me, I cannot get myself to go topless during sex because I am almost positive it will turn him off (not to mention the immense embarrassment it would cause me). It bothers him when I keep my shirt on, however; he resents making this compromise for my own comfort.

I do not know how to handle this; it has affected every aspect of my life. I get uncomfortable with him in public or when we watch a movie, because breasts have become America's most public private parts; they bombard us everywhere we turn!

I have talked to him about getting breast implants (uh, for me). He finds that detestable, he says, and nothing but a turnoff. His story is different when it comes to Pamela Anderson and the like. Plus the fact that he looks at pornography does not make things any easier for me.

Thank you.

P.S. If you're planning to advise me to talk to him and work it out through communication, don't bother—that has never worked. Some words of advice would be much appreciated.

**A** Your husband needs to have breast-reduction surgery—from his brain! Tell him his breast obsession is disrespectful of his wife and of his marriage, and that you want him to stop. If he won't, insist that he see a marital therapist with you. Otherwise your marriage is headed for defeat on this battleground of body parts.

It's also possible that you need to quit bullying your own

boobs. Yes, we live in a culture that worships breasts—and wealth, and youth, and happiness, possessions, and perfection.

Get my drift? The universe offers us infinite ways to torture ourselves, and you seem determined to sample every one. The cover girl with the perfect bod is a myth of media manufacture. If you have to regret something, regret our collective acceptance of this myth, not the "fact" that you happen not to conform to some aspect of it. Women living in the real world, meanwhile, choose to focus on the positive aspects of their bodies and their lives.

I don't think implants are the answer to your prayers. I think the real problem may be your self-hatred. With shame comes anger. My guess is that you're furious with your husband for witnessing your pain.

If you can't voluntarily shunt these feelings aside, I urge you to talk with a therapist about your self-loathing and to consult a doctor about the potential usefulness of an antidepressant medication. Body detesting, irritability, unceasing anger—all classic symptoms of untreated depression.

From a diagnostic standpoint, depression has a distinctively obsessive quality to it. You're on your way to a gold medal in the event.

The objective truth is that your husband thinks you look just fine. With time and some professional help, you may eventually come to appreciate his view of your landscape— not as flat as Kansas, but a physiognomy of soft curves and subtle beauty.

# 8

# Missing in Action

**Q** Hello! I hope you can help me with my situation.

I am a healthy 51-year-old—5'4", 120 pounds—and have been married for 27 years. As with most couples, our sex life was hot and steamy and wonderful at first. As the years went by, though, my husband became less and less in the mood. Then, about two years ago, he told me that he just wasn't attracted to me anymore. He still loves me, he says, and he does act that way—except for the sex.

We have a good relationship. We share many interests and activities, and we enjoy being together.

I asked him if there was anything I could do to make myself more attractive. He said he didn't think that would help. Although I consider myself average-looking, other men do find me attractive.

He denies having a relationship with anyone else, nor do I see any sign of that happening. When he gets an urge for sex, he told me, he just masturbates. I am having a hard time accepting he would rather do that than have sex with me.

He refuses to go for counseling. I have tried to accept this situation, but I have normal sexual urges and don't want my sex life to be over. So... can you help?

**A** Unlike death and taxes, lifetime sex is no certainty. What newly married couple, transported by the throes of passion, could possibly foresee the onset of this dilemma? And yet it happens.

"Small comfort in that," you snort—and I agree, so let's review the clues and point you toward some help with your Lone Ranger lover.

Your husband's wilting interest in sex (for two, that is) could have any number of causes. Some people are raised to believe that partnered sex should taper off after the procreative years. Perhaps your husband was brought up this way?

If not, think back to the time when sex was good, then gradually diminished. What else may have faded around that time? Did he begin to resist trying new activities? If so, you may have made many unconscious accommodations that are visible only in life's rearview mirror. He may be more "Herman the Hermit" than you'd care to admit.

Reading between the lines, the biggest cause for concern is that he is not curious about how you feel. His lack of concern about your feelings is a clue that something has shifted inside him. He is not quite the guy you married. This may stem from depression or some other psychiatric problem. It may be the effect of aging on his particular personality type. It may even be an early sign of dementia, such as early-onset Alzheimer's disease.

Another clue is that your husband does not lack sexual drive, but he has lost interest in sharing a physical connection with you. To begin finding out why, urge him to get a complete physical—including a check of his testosterone, thyroid, and cortisol levels. Seek out a physician familiar with the problems of older adults. Accompany your husband to the exam, then speak privately to the physician. If he or she thinks a medication could help, tell your husband you expect him to try this for the sake of your marriage.

A spouse who resists counseling will occasionally relent if the recommendation comes from a health professional. It's certainly worth having the doctor give this a try as well.

Even if you figure out precisely what is wrong, be prepared for your husband to refuse the suggested treatment. One way around this is a little old-fashioned horse trading: "We've tried it your way for X number of months/years," you can say. "Now let's try it my way for a month." Or: "You don't have to do this forever, but I would like you to agree to try it for three months."

If your husband rejects all interventions, you will know you've reached a pivot point. Seek counseling alone. It will give you a place to grieve, to review your options, and to figure out ways to boost your involvement with friends.

To lift the siege once and for all, try one of these proven success strategies from my own clinical experience:

*Remain calm and firm.*

*Avoid shame or blame.*

*State clearly that things cannot continue as they are.*

Those steps may sound simple, but each one takes time to take effect. Until that happens—until the castle walls crumble down—don't neglect to take good care of yourself.

**Q** I have been married for 23 years. My husband is a wonderful—some might even say unusual—man: He does dishes and laundry, cooks, & fixes things (the right way). We share a lot of the same interests. He is intelligent & warm, with a loving heart, and he loves me very much.

So... my problem?

We have not been intimate for the past 15 years.

We have been to counseling more than once. He says he is afraid of not being able to please me. His parents did not have an intimate relationship.

Whenever he says he will try something, he conveniently forgets about it. If I make the first move, he cannot get an erection. We were once told to try massages first; I am still waiting for mine. He will touch me with clothing on, but not my naked skin.

I do not know what to do anymore... please help!

**A** Your situation is a poignant reminder that human beings are complex creatures, especially in relationships. You find him warm and caring, but he's left you out in the cold when it comes to sexual affection. The reasons for his reluctance to be skin-to-skin do not seem readily apparent. You've already shown patience—and then some! Now you will need to add determination to fix things—the right way.

First, the positives: You feel he loves you. That's good, given that most people want a sexual relationship based on love and mutual respect. And he likes to please you outside the bedroom—another plus.

Next, the challenges: When you initiate sex, he experiences erectile difficulties. Massages are hardly a two-way street, and he'd just as soon you kept your clothes on, thank you very much. One condition your shrinking violet does not suffer from is inconsistency; it's clear that he routinely shuns close physical interaction. The question is why?

You have options, none of them effortless. You can continue as you've been doing and "enjoy" a pleasant but sexless marriage. Many people would make that choice, and there's nothing wrong with it. If you're one of them, you can try to content yourself with masturbation and the kinds of physical contact you know he is comfortable giving.

If you find self-satisfaction less than satisfactory, however, you'll want to seek professional help from a sex therapist—a mental health professional who has been specially trained to understand human sexuality and the myriad problems that arise from sexual functioning. Get ready for a battle royale—but hold your ground. If he refuses to cooperate, go by yourself; ask the sex therapist to help you figure him out (and how to figure him into the conversation).

An evaluation of your problems will address the avoidance of sexual intimacy. An anxiety disorder may be causing your husband's apathy. Negative reactions to sexual closeness based on something from his past could also be to blame. His reactions might just as likely stem from his recognition that he is not attracted to women, but doesn't want to leave the marriage or come out as a gay man.

All speculation, of course, will remain just that until the two of you get a professional's opinion.

Here's a final thought about what might be going on. Your husband may have a neurologic processing disorder known as Sensory Defensiveness, or SD. This condition affects the way the brain handles sensory input, making it difficult for the person to modulate a response to situations considered normal by others. Persons with SD may experience (normally) pleasurable touch as the sensory equivalent of fingernails on a chalkboard. They may also be hypersensitive to ambient noise (music in the apartment next door, for example) or strong or unusual odors (that patchouli oil worn by your fellow commuters in Seattle).

Certain sensations—the wetness of open-mouth kissing, the stroking of genitals—can also trigger SD. On occasion, an SD sufferer may get squeamish over skin or touch. Some people with SD may even grow anxious at the mere anticipation of experiencing sensory input.

You can read about Sensory Defensiveness and its most effective treatments in Sharon Heller's excellent book, *Too Loud, Too Bright, Too Fast, Too Tight*. Or visit www.temple.edu/OT/Neuro_Behavioral_Center2.htm.

A problem 15 years in the making will take more than 15 minutes to mend. To find a sex therapist near you, consult the website of the American Association of Sex Educators, Counselors, and Therapists at www.aasect.org. Persuading your husband to physically attend a counseling session may be a different matter altogether. But be kind, be determined, and persevere; together the two of you should be able to find if not a solution then at least a mutually acceptable accommodation.

## 9

# Wander Lust

I am 37 years old and my husband is 36. We have been married for 10 years. We had dated for eight years before that, with a breakup (which was my fault) that lasted about a year after we had been going out for six years.

Although we have never cheated on each other while married, I was a bit of a run-around at times before we got married. Since then, I have been totally his, and I am interested in absolutely no one but him.

Just recently my friend thought it would be funny to play a joke on him by instant messaging him and talking sexy.

I couldn't do that to him, so I warned him what was coming. He then decided to play the joke on her. They talked nasty for a few days by IM and she sent me the messages so I could see what was being said.

I tried to put it in its place—a joke—but hearing that my husband's favorite is big boobs (I know men love them, but I don't have them) and that he was going to enjoy doing all sorts of things to her was just like kicking me in the face.

Since then I have found out that he fantasizes about other women and doing things with them. He says it is normal and healthy for people to fantasize. I don't know about that. I fantasize about him alone and honestly cannot think of a single time when I dreamed of another man doing things to me. It feels like I would be cheating if I did.

I am having a difficult time dealing with this. I feel like his fantasizing is a step toward doing something like cheating. I guess I just need to know if it is normal for people to fantasize about other people they aren't with.

Thank you for your time. And please help—I feel I am crazy.

**A** You're not crazy—but don't you think you and your husband did something that is?

People on sitcoms can do these sorts of things and untangle them by next week's episode. For people in real life, however, everything has consequences. You and your husband will be eating these leftovers long after the concoction you created has gone stale.

Here's my crash course in fantasy and its side effects: Sexual dreaming and sexual daydreams are both perfectly normal. The human brain, even deep in sleep, can have arousing fantasies—and these can certainly be naughty rather than nice.

For some people, fantasies create a high level of discomfort. For others, they're low-cost entertainment: They bring pleasure, increase erotic focus, and require no viewing screen.

Every individual tends to have her or his own favorite thing(s) to savor in the privacy of her or his own cranium. Some people fantasize only about their mate; others let their minds conjure a wide array of imaginary partners. Look at former president Jimmy Carter: In a *Playboy* magazine interview he confessed to committing "lust in my heart," yet he wound up with a Nobel Peace Prize.

From a clinical standpoint, fantasy is a commonplace sex-therapy technique. It is often employed to help people heighten their sexual arousal while masturbating. In fact, many couples report they have no problem if their partner fantasizes during sex—just so long as the dream person remains only that.

Some people fret that an individual can get hooked on fantasy, preferring make-believe lover to the real deal. The same tired trope has been trotted out for years about women who use vibrators—the fear being that a woman will lose interest in nonpowered pulsation.

When a couple is loving, respectful, and communicates well in their sexual life, no prop can compete with the real McCoy. For most, fantasy is an imaginary act that hurts no one. But as you found out when your "friend" funneled you those "instant massages" authored by your husband, a fantasy can inflict lasting emotional wounds.

Humans are curious creatures, drawn toward that which

is dangerous. Our brains get a rush from doing something that our conscience deems to be over the edge: Just look at how many "rational" human beings hang glide, bungee jump, and invest their money in the stock market.

By the same flame-gazing token, the mere fact of knowing that one's partner fantasizes can be arousing. For more adventurous couples, hearing one's partner describe how those fantasies unfold can be a source of sexual stimulation—even sexual satisfaction.

Yet there's a limit to conjecture: A couple can misuse fantasies, inflating them from idle scenarios into supposed wishes as a means of increasing sexual tension. Like gamblers gone wild, they keep upping the ante until they've wagered more capital than they own.

You and your husband began innocently enough. Now you must face up to the fact that things got out of hand. Take responsibility for the misadventure, then work to rebuild your connection to one another. And take heart: You made a mistake, not a nuclear warhead.

**Q** I've been with my husband for nine years, and I think he's seeing another woman. How can I find out for sure?

**A** It's possible to imagine infidelities, especially if a partner has cheating on his résumé. But I've never known a suspicious husband or wife who was completely wrong. Spousal radar is a reliable instrument. A mate may be having drinks with a colleague instead of earth-shattering orgasms, but we rarely conjure fears from nothing.

Test your intuition before dropping the bomb on him. Look for odd changes in behavior, says private investigator

Anthony DeLorenzo, author of *28 Tell-Tale Signs of a Cheating Spouse*. Has your husband lost interest in sex? Or conversely, has he busted out a new move after years of the usual routine? If he used to mope after an argument, does he now take a drive? Does the phone bill disappear?

You've got to air your mistrust, or it will poison your marriage. When you confront him, your best shot for honesty is to sound concerned, not angry or accusational. Sit down with him and gently say, "I've been worried that you're seeing someone else." Some stray cats will confess instantly. Others may blow up in anger or offer flimsy denials.

If your gut isn't satisfied, ask him to see a counselor with you. If he agrees, there's a good chance he's clean. Only a ruthless egomaniac would undergo therapy to help you deal with unfounded suspicions that are not, in fact, unfounded.

The only way to be dead sure is to hire a private investigator (the yellow pages can point you to several). You might find that he really is volunteering at the soup kitchen. But even if you learn the worst, hard evidence of adultery can protect your legal and financial interests during a divorce. Please don't tail him yourself. You're too emotionally invested to be lurking behind the azaleas. Besides, private eyes have better recording devices.

**Q** I recently discovered that my husband of 15 years has been e-mailing a woman he met a few months ago. She confides intimate details of her relationship with other men, asks for his advice, and talks about how much she values his "friendship." She also questions why he never mentions his wife. Should I confront him about this "secret" relationship?

A Unless you're married to Dr. Phil, your husband is getting more from his covert cavorting than the altruism rush of dispensing sound counsel. He's indulging in virtual voyeurism—and by flaunting with flair, she's enabling him.

Perhaps I'm wrong; perhaps your husband really is auditioning a new set of friends. What's beyond conjecture, however, is that cyberspace abounds with surreptitious spouses—and that he has stumbled onto a modern-day Mae West. Their e-mail exchanges are not so much "talk" as titillation.

Let's devise a plan to resolve your marital troubles. We'll start with a refresher course in Internet usage. Call it Virtueless Reality 101.

The Internet is both a treasure chest and a trash dump. Many people go there with a specific (and non-skanky) goal in mind: They want to buy a certain book, book a seat to a certain destination, or track down a certain fact that will complete their Ph.D. thesis (or daily crossword puzzle). Other people, however, go to the Net to see what will turn up: They sweep cyberspace with their mental detectors, hoping to uncover a buzz. They choose fantasy over reality—and expect to elude detection by hiding the booty.

The expert on Internet abuse is Dr. Kimberly Young of Pittsburgh. Her two books—*Caught in the Net: How to Recognize the Signs of Internet Addiction* and *Tangled in the Web: Understanding Cybersex from Fantasy to Addiction*—are indispensable primers on what has become an underground plague. Convenience, anonymity, and escape draw people to the Internet, says Dr. Young. That escape may take the form of sexual thrills, or it may entail a more metaphorical release—from pressures, from fears, from real-life problems.

As you've discovered, though, the thrills are far from free—they're costing you big time. It's time to stop the flame drain and salvage the marriage.

Before you take him to task, take stock of what you've got: Are you satisfied with the level of intimacy, communication, and sexual expression the two of you share? If not, get ready to invest in some real-life growing up as a result of pulling the plug on fantasyland.

Tell him your role as the "never-mentioned" wife just ended. Explain that, acting on a hunch, you did some snooping that revealed his alter e-go. If he is embarrassed and apologetic, he may indeed have made a colossal blunder that has left him older and wiser. In that case, his eagerness to make amends will go a long way toward putting the incident behind you. And get through this hard time you will, just as you survived those 3:13 a.m. phone calls from your teenagers, or that year the neighbors bred the pit bulls.

If he acts fortified rather than mortified at your detective work, however, you're dealing with a mistake of a different make. Remain unmoved by any accusations of duplicity; that sort of phony self-righteousness will only distract you from the hard work—and clear choices—ahead. Either she goes or he goes—out the door.

In short, this cyber-relationship must be killed in order to keep your own flesh-and-blood relationship alive. Ask him—no, direct him—to end it and erase all saved files.

Purging his human hard drive, though, may take much longer. I suggest you both read *Tangled in the Web* and talk about the everyday pressures that make fantasy and escapism so intoxicatingly appealing. Discuss each person's triggers for feeling vulnerable, unappreciated, or stressed out. With a bit of luck and a realistic shoulder to life's wheel, you may be able to redesign your lives so that he gets more out of reality—and you both get more out of your marriage.

# 10

# Deal Breakers

**Q** My live-in companion of three years wants to get married, but I don't really see any benefits in it. I've been married before and so has she, and I don't see how it will change our day-to-day lives. She says it will make her feel more secure. Why is this such a big deal?

**A** Not exactly Mr. Romance, are you? Marriage is not a business decision where you carefully measure pros and cons. Even if it were, there are plenty of legal and financial pluses to putting a ring on her finger. The most important?

Laws vary from state to state, but in many, husbands and wives can make medical decisions for each other, whereas unmarried partners cannot.

Some other technicalities may interest you as well. For example, your wife can't be forced to testify against you in court, but the feds can make unbetrothed sing like a canary. And if you get jail time, a wife is often accorded more visitation leeway than a mate. Just a couple of tidbits for you to consider there!

At the same time you're wondering why getting married is such a big deal to her, she's wondering why resisting it is such a big deal to you. Reverse roles: How would you feel if you wanted to get married and she didn't really see the point of publicly affirming your devotion to each other? Gives you pause, doesn't it?

Maybe she's just eager to use a wonderful phrase: "my husband." If you love this woman—and that's a big if— marry her. Why? For no other reason than she wants you to, and a woman's entitled to want that. In fact, don't just marry her. Make her feel that winning her hand makes you a very lucky man.

**Q** I have discovered that my partner recently reposted his personal ad on the Internet. He has been looking at and e-mailing (and I'm not sure what else) other women.

He calls this an innocent pastime that keeps him from getting bored. I say he's cheating—not just on me, but on the women he's talking to online. We broke up over this once before.

Best advice: Dump him? Or let him continue—and start to play the same game he is?

A Posting a personal ad on the Internet is as subtle as advertising on the Goodyear Blimp at the Rose Bowl. He's broadcasting a message to the world, and it says, "Hey, girls—I'm available!"

Your partner's choice of how to solve his "boredom" is revealing. It speaks volumes about his character that he has opted not to venture out into the world and volunteer for a good cause; instead he has elected to give of himself by, well, other means. The next poster child for civic involvement he's not.

I suppose you can consider yourself fortunate, in a way: This is a glimpse into his soul you might never have gleaned from reading the most in-depth personal ad he has posted online.

Which leads me to ask: How did you discover this peccadillo on his part? It sounds like you've been involved in your own undercover investigation. If this is the case, you've got the goods—so knock off the 007 routine, already! Nothing further will be gained, and you run the risk of funneling your fury into pointlessly gathering more evidence of his transgressions. Remember, every confirmed masochist is looking for a sadist, so squelch your martyrly urges. Some couples play the game of cat and mouse without end, guaranteeing that they will live miserably ever after.

I will say one thing for your partner, however: The man is consistent—consistently foolish, that is. Identical behavior on his part has already caused you to leave him once. Now it's up to you to decide whether you want to stay with a man who treats you this way. (Can you guess which way I'm leaning?)

If you leave him, be prepared for his blimp to deflate. He'll be surprised—nay, wounded—that you "misunderstood his intentions." But his tears are those of a crocodile; he's shedding them for himself, and for the comfort of that comfy chair that lets him roam without ever leaving his computer.

Should you level the playing field by stooping to the same game? Unadvisable: Where there's duplicity there are no winners. My advice is to dump this loser and get back in the game of life.

**Q** Are there sensitivity reasons for older couples to choose not to use condoms?

**A** That all depends—how sensitive are you to disease and death?

There is no age at which sexually active people do not run the risk of contracting STIs, or sexually transmitted infections: HIV/AIDS, herpes, HPV/genital warts, gonorrhea, chlamydia, syphilis, and hepatitis B, to name a few, are all passed along through unprotected—that is to say, condom-free—sexual behavior.

Just in case that catalogue of medical calamities doesn't put fear in your heart (and a condom on your member), let me spell things out for you: Modern couples use condoms because STIs are rampant in modern society. True sensitivity in today's sexual universe therefore means respecting your partner's sexual health, not selfishly maximizing your own enjoyment.

The inside of a woman's vagina is a mucous membrane like the interior lining of your cheek. The fact that viruses and infections can penetrate a membrane more easily than skin makes the price of unprotected sex higher for a woman than it is for a man: Women are twice as likely to get genital warts; they are three times as likely to get herpes.

Many STIs are "silent." You can become infected but remain asymptomatic, prompting you to pass the infection unwittingly to a partner.

For all its currency, the term "safe sex" is something of a misnomer. It popularly describes the use of condoms to prevent conception and STIs, yet the only surefire way to avoid both conditions is to abstain from genital contact altogether.

When inaugurating a new sexual relationship (at no matter what age), have an honest talk with your partner about his or her history of known STIs. Get tested to determine if either one of you has HIV/AIDS. Condoms are necessary to provide further protection against that welter of sexual afflictions I mentioned at the top of this answer.

Now that I've disclosed such intimate advice about your sexual behavior, I feel comfortable divulging my favorite oxymorons:

Working vacation

Jumbo shrimp

Military intelligence

Microsoft Works

Postal service

Scottish food

Condom "choice"

See what I'm getting at here? When it comes to condom use, I am virulently anti-choice—and you should be too!

Okay, now let's tackle that sensitivity issue that is so

obviously bedeviling you. If covering up deprives you of too much sensation, switch to an ultrathin latex condom, or try using the polyurethane type; these are costlier but conduct heat, permitting more natural sensation during intercourse. To increase comfort and reduce the odds of breakage, don't forget to add a water-based lubricant.

If you favor the activist approach to sex, the magazine *Consumer Reports* reviews a panoply of condom brands every few years. This allows you to compare and contrast different models that may resolve your sensitivity issues. Alternatively or in addition, ask your partner to keep stroking supersensitive parts of your anatomy, such as buttocks or scrotum, to heighten stimulation during intercourse.

Condoms—ribbed or ruby red, make them part of your performance package! In time (and with testing), you may both grow confident that neither one of you has brought any excess baggage, so to speak, into the relationship. Then—and only then—can you take it all off and still be a sensitive man.

**Q** Although I have seen two therapists for the relationship problem I'm about to reveal, it still gnaws at me. So here's one more stab at resolving it objectively.

Five years ago my husband passed away. I was 50 at the time. He had been ill for several years and it was very difficult for both of us, but we stayed together, and we actually had a good relationship in the last few years of his life.

At the time he passed away, I thought I would never want another relationship. Now, however, I have very little family (an adult son and stepchildren who all live in different states) and would very much like to be in a stable relationship or married.

After about eight months of being a widow, I was extremely lonely and impulsively answered a personal ad in a local magazine. A man called me and it was instant attraction for both of us. Then, slowly, I found out he was addicted to hard-core porn. Despite this—and I tried to get out of the relationship several times—things "progressed" and I fell in love with him. He moved in with me the following year.

I do not approve of porn, and I tried to prohibit it. He also had a drinking problem and anger issues. Life was tumultuous, to say the least. Finally, I ended the relationship—the hardest thing I ever did—and he moved out. I was so distraught that several of my friends thought I would end up in a psychiatric unit.

I then read every book on addiction and relationships I could find. I also joined Al-Anon, got therapy, and dated other men. That process opened my eyes to the fact that I had become addicted to this man—and that I am still addicted to him. Sometimes I think it would be easier for me to get hooked on heroin and give it up than to ever go through this again.

Now here it is over two years later and I still miss him terribly. The one time I saw him during that time, it was clear that neither my feelings nor his behaviors had changed. Even though he loved me too, I know it would have meant a lifetime of hardship to marry him.

I have dated two other men since him. Neither relationship worked out. I do not want to give up trying to find someone new, but this issue is overburdening my heart.

How do I get over this feeling of loss? I think about him

every day. I still want to see him again. But it would be very risky for me to do this, so I have not contacted him.

I have tried telling myself every reason I can think of as to why this would never work out. (I take an antidepressant, but I think there's more to this than a matter of depression.) I am a professional and have a master's degree in my field of work, but I feel incapable of applying reason to my own situation.

I'd like to hear your opinion on this matter. I have never suffered such relationship pain and fear this will haunt me the rest of my life. I think about moving to shed the memories, but this is not financially feasible; also, it would mean leaving my good friends in the area.

**A** You ask if you can resolve this problem objectively and the answer is "no." This is an entirely personal, subjective problem. There is no single piece of advice from me—nor is there any specific act on your part—guaranteed to help you "get over it." If this was about pulling yourself up by your bootstraps, you are certainly smart enough and willing enough to have done that already.

Your head has told you the right things to do, but your heart resists them. Medicine such as antidepressants can be an aid, but it cannot banish the extent of your depression and pain.

At the risk of sounding like Yoda, complicated indeed is your relationship with this man—but not for the reasons you think. He isn't so very complex. He's actually one-dimensional, and transparently manipulative to boot. He's in it only for himself.

Far less clear is what he has come to mean to you, and

how you can progress beyond your current misery.

Your willingness to "hold on" well beyond the emotionally healthy (and physically safe) limit is probably rooted in your past experiences with others, including your earliest life experiences. All children develop what psychologists call "internal working models of attachment," which are shaped over time by the ways in which parents and other important people treat the child. This early set of attachments forms the basis of how you expect to be treated by others throughout your life—including how you treat yourself.

Everyone possesses an internal psychological life in which good relationships and unhealthy relationships repeat aspects of their past. Perhaps it is unconscious, but this man got under your skin and you are replaying some old theme. This theme includes your expectation of loneliness and perhaps even punishment.

Although you say you have tried counseling, my guess is that your impatience with your pain caused you to quit before you were done. You need to return to counseling. This time, make sure you find a therapist who works psychodynamically with clients. That process is rooted in the understanding that early experiences of hurt or disappointment can spark conflict later on—conflict such as ending up with a man whom you know to be "bad medicine." There is nothing short or sweet about your problem; in order for therapy to work, you must make a long-term commitment to the process.

You've had much to grieve about in your life—a challenging marriage, the death of your husband, this recent rocky relationship. Your obsession with Mr. Wrong is like an addiction to suffering. Although it hasn't been healthy, it has at least filled the void of loss you've experienced. Remember, you don't have a relationship with him; you do have a relationship with punishing yourself, and a relationship with suffering. You will remain locked in this torturous cycle until you break it yourself by seeking relief via professional help.

# 11

# Divorce and Its Aftermath

**Q** Two years ago, my husband left me for another woman after 33 years of marriage. Now he says he made a mistake and wants to come back. He seems sincere, but I don't know how we could simply pick up where we left off. Should I trust him?

**A** Joni Mitchell got it right: "You don't know what you got 'til it's gone."

"It's common for a spouse to regret breaking up a long-term marriage," says Linda Newhart Lotz, Ph.D., a licensed psychologist and AASECT-certified sex therapist in Gainesville, Florida. "They leave in search of excitement and then miss the companionship and support."

If you still love him, it must be tempting to hope you can forget this. Besides, who among us doesn't love it when they come crawling back? I still fantasize that the guy who dumped me in high school will track me down and beg me to forgive him.

But be careful. "It's not a good idea to take him back out of a codependent instinct," says Lotz. "Many women have an urge to make everybody else happy." Figure out if he has learned anything and has a new appreciation of you.

Of course, if he's still living with the other woman, he needs to move out before you two talk any further. Suggesting couples therapy can make him show his cards. If he balks, that's a bad sign; he should be humbled and solicitous of you. If he's not, it could be wiser to move on.

**Q** My boyfriend, Tony, and I have been living together for five years, and I have told him I would like to be married to him. The problem is that he and his last wife never got divorced, even though they have been split up over 10 years. They promised her mother on her deathbed that they would never get divorced (they are Catholic).

They don't plan on ever getting back together again. They have two grown children together.

Should I be content to just live with him right now? Or should I give him an ultimatum: Either he gets divorced so we can get married or I'm leaving him? I love him very much—he's really good to me—but I feel like I'm being cheated out of the security I should be entitled to as his mate.

A Tony sounds like a real tiger; he has a way of treating you that's just GRR-R-Reat! But he's treating his mate the same way he treats his faith—his commitment does not quite go "all the way."

I know it worked stellarly for Tracy and Hepburn—all that love, none of those pesky obligations—but Good Lady Katharine may have had a far lower security quotient than most people seek.

The vast majority of (non-screen-siren) women would say that you've been more than patient enough. Five years is a long time to live with someone—long enough, for example, for me to predict that the two of you will go right on living together, with no significant change in your marital status.

And now a confession of my own: Forgive me, sister, but I cannot comprehend the morality of this tale. These are the facts as I perceive them:

Tony is happy to be a Catholic who is estranged from his wife but lives with another woman.

Tony would be unhappy to be a divorced Catholic.

Tony is happy to make unrealistic deathbed promises, notably to other (and, apparently, truly committed) Catholics.

You and Tony face nothing but hard choices ahead. If he divorces his wife, he must face up to his religion and his conscience—that is, the memory of his sainted mother-in-law. If you leave him, you will grieve.

Let me ask you a question that I hope will crystallize your connubial conundrum: How can the two of you face each other over your morning breakfast cereal? Sugar coating or no, I could not play this charade.

**Q** My boyfriend is divorced and has a couple of children, who live in another state. Every time he has any contact with them, they make him feel guilty about them not being together.

He doesn't deal with the guilt very well. In fact, he takes it out on me.

How can I make him see they are manipulating him to get whatever they want from him? This is really taking a toll on our relationship.

**A** No one enters a marriage expecting to get divorced, but that's the fate of 40 to 50 percent of first-time marriages. (The figures are even higher for second marriages and up). As a doctor friend puts it, "Would you consent to an elective surgery with a success rate of 50 percent?" Not bloody likely! Yet we blithely shove off in the good ship Marriage nonetheless, confident that we'll weather all storms, have our kids, and make landfall on that distant shore, our craft still solid beneath our feet.

The reality is otherwise.

Divorce is like a death that produces no corpse but a great deal of mourning. Although most people are anxious to get over their divorce, few of them anticipate the extent of the need to tend the other bonds disrupted by it. These include each parent's ties to their children—in this case, your boyfriend's relationship with his children far away.

This sort of healing is hard work. It requires patience and a long-term perspective.

Here's my advice for your boyfriend:

Erma Bombeck, that muse of the mundane, once called guilt "the gift that keeps on giving."

If you see her point—if, that is, you're feeling guilty that you can't be more involved in your kids' lives—own up to it. Then take responsibility for changing the situation. If, on the other hand, you're channeling your guilt into mentally berating yourself and your girlfriend, I'll have to conclude you're less concerned with solving problems than savoring pain. Try counseling to help you face up to your responsibilities.

Please don't believe that your kids enjoy manipulating you. If you have been a Disney dad until now, feeding them only candy, try bolstering your relationship with solid inter-actions: Contact them regularly by phone; write frequent e-mails; make face-to-face visits where you work together on their next book report or math assignment.

All children need to have limits set for them—and all children resent it. But if you are putting money in their college funds rather than financing one more trip to Chuck E. Cheese, you won't feel torn. Treat them with love, patience, steadiness, and the gift of your time.

And here's my advice for you:

It sounds like you are dating a package deal there, not just a person. When your boyfriend's marital vessel sank, it left survivors with all kinds of needs and feelings. If his children are between the ages of 0 and 19, he owes them constant contact. He needs to devote his primary time and resources to raising his kids.

But you do have choices. If you are convinced he is the love of your life, taking the long view will redound to your benefit. Support him in caring for his children. Develop perspective—and a boatload of your own interests, hobbies, and friendships to occupy your time while he is busy caring for his kids.

If this seems unappealing, stop to think that his current problem—dealing with guilt by dishing it out on you—may betray a much deeper issue. George Santayana, had he been an advice columnist rather than a poet/philosopher/social critic—oh wait, they're the same thing, aren't they?—might have put it this way: "Those who do not remember their past relationships are condemned to relive them."

So sometime soon—why not make it right after you finish reading this?—please get clarity on precisely how your boyfriend may have contributed to the dissolution of his marriage.

**Q** Is it crazy to get a divorce but to keep living together in the same house?

**A** If you're still a couple and are considering getting a divorce for some financial reason—such as to qualify for certain benefits—proceed cautiously. This is a complicated matter, and you can attract more trouble than you're anticipating, even if you think you have all the details squared away. "Divorce has many financial ramifications concerning things such as pensions, estates, life insurance, disability insurance, and wills," says Richard F. Barry of San Rafael, California, president of the American Academy of Matrimonial Lawyers. You'll also lose some spousal rights in serious medical situations. Finally, the IRS doesn't take kindly to sham divorces, says Barry. "They have a way of piercing what they consider to be tax dodges."

If you're divorcing because you truly want to end your marriage but cannot yet afford to move out (this happens much more frequently than you might imagine), get a legal separation agreement that spells out issues such as how bills will be divided, says Dana Breslin, an elder-law attorney in Brookhaven, Pennsylvania.

Finally, if you're staying under the same roof to avoid hassles by keeping certain financial arrangements the same, I'd likewise expect problems. You may both be supportive of each other now, but what happens when he suddenly wants to sell his half of the house and move to Jersey with your old Avon rep?

If you're getting divorced emotionally, get divorced financially as well. If you then choose to help each other, great. But for legal concerns, true independence is a better idea.

**Q** Our marriage ended two years ago, but my ex-husband and I still sleep together—often. I've heard this type of thing is pretty common, and we both enjoy it, but I'm not sure whether it's smart to continue doing this. Would I be wise to stop seeing him?

**A** It's not unusual for ex-husbands and ex-wives to have sex. On a purely practical level, lots of us have strong sex drives, and few of us have dozens of dance partners on speed dial. Moreover, even though the marriage didn't endure, there is often a legacy of affection.

But for most, post-split passion is more likely occasional, as in the New Year's Eve quickie for old times' sake. You mention that your sex-with-your-ex is a steady thing, and that can bring up other issues.

I won't vote against free-agent, clear-eyed adults using their skills to bestow pleasure on each other. But if you're uneasy, ask yourself some questions. First, if you're looking for a new relationship, is canoodling with your ex holding you back from finding a new man? After all, cuddling with him gives you all the benefits of physical intimacy without the tedious work a brand new man would require.

Second, although it's technically possible to have sex without emotional involvement, it doesn't happen often. "Even if you're dating other men, you may not be fully open to another full-fledged love," says Jeanne Shaw, Ph.D., a clinical psychologist and sex therapist from Atlanta. "And, of course, not many men will want to date a woman who's sleeping with her ex."

All this said, if you've looked into your heart and don't think sweating with your oldie is holding you in the past, there's no real reason why you two shouldn't love, honor, and cherish each other 'til the break of day.

# 12

# All in the Family

**Q** My boyfriend and I live 140 miles apart, and we each have our own home. How can we get to the point of having a satisfying relationship? My boyfriend has family members living with him.

**A** Your question leaves me feeling unsatisfied, so we're both in the same boat! Taking your statements at face value, however, I'd advise the following:

If he is the love of your life, consider relocating to be near him.

If the relationship is too new for predictions, set up a regular schedule of visits and let things unfold from there.

If spending time together when other family members are in the house makes you uncomfortable, then—as his kids might say—"Get a room, you two!" (That's "room" as in "motel room.")

If you need permission from someone else to do any of the above, I hereby grant it. That and $3.75 will buy you a cappuccino (your costs may vary).

Dating as an adult is no simple matter. It's nothing like it was back in high school, when curfews and coifs were your concerns of highest consequence. Adult relationships must be conducted by partners who are simultaneously trying to negotiate a three-dimensional minefield of competing responsibilities, from demanding jobs to challenging kids to needy older relatives to leaky bladders to houses that won't sell. (Pause here to catch your breath. Now name out loud the first concern that enters your mind; it's highly likely that *that* concern will attempt to sabotage your newfound love at some point in the months ahead.)

I read something else between the lines of your question, though: Is it possible you disapprove of your boyfriend's living situation? This might be because he has older children who you feel should be launched in life by now, or because you resent the presence of his older relatives who cannot live independently.

John Donne may have been getting at something similar nearly 400 years ago, when he wrote in his *Meditation XVII* that "No man is an island, entire of itself; every man is a piece of the continent, a part of the main." Pursuing that line of thought, you need to look inside your heart and acknowledge that every person is a package deal. Because your new relationship does not exist in isolation, your boyfriend is unlikely to quit the continent of his emotions and desires in order to live exclusively on your own little island.

**Q** My parents have been married for 50 years, but a series of strokes have left my mother a semi-invalid. Missing the active sex life they once shared, my father asked me to set him up with a willing sex partner.

He is serious—and I am scandalized. What can I do for (or should I say "do about") him? This subject is not comfortable for me. What do you suggest to older men who are in his position?

**A** I take it you and your father haven't had that "little talk" just yet. You know—the one that goes, "Dad, you're right: Sex is one of life's great joys. There was a time when people thought that sex existed solely for creating terrific offspring (like me). But now we know that it's a pleasurable part of living at any age. You and Mom were lucky to enjoy such a healthy sex life together for such a lengthy period of time. It's sad for both of you that these strokes have robbed Mom of her health.

"I know you miss what you had, Dad, but I'm beginning to wonder what's going on in that noggin of yours. I mean, get a grip! Two key parts of healthy sexuality are good judgment and solid boundaries: Your sex life should be private, so I'm not going to be your Dr. Ruth or your dating service."

A daughter can't be a best friend, a counselor, or a confessor. Now that you have his attention, go on to suggest the following options that he can pursue without your involvement:

First, your parents can visit a sex therapist. Given two willing partners, many mutually satisfying accommodations can be made in sexual activity.

Second, if your mother is unable to participate, your father can go alone to discuss his problems—including his frustration over unmet needs. This is clearly a case where professional—not familial—help is going to be required to sort out his options.

**Q** I have been dating the same man now for the last 10 years. He is totally devoted to his mother, who has a live-in boyfriend; he therefore takes care of them both. Having recently retired, I would now like to travel, but he says he cannot leave his mother "home alone" for more than two days.

Am I being unfair to want to go my own way? I feel he is simply waiting for someone younger to come along—and using his mother as an excuse.

**A** And here I thought we'd gotten all the mileage we could out of the phrase "momma's boy"!

He's not waiting for someone younger—he's in love with someone older. He's tied to his mother, and has been for the entire decade you've dated him.

Home Boy has never really been your man, and now that you finally have some free time to enjoy each other, you're seeing him for who he truly is: He has other priorities; he's not going to change; he has not loved you as wholeheartedly as you have loved him.

## ···When Kids Are········
# IN THE HOUSE

**S**ingle parent Catherine Daley had a dilemma:
How to balance her desire for intimacy with the
men she dated with her need to model responsible
behavior for her three teenagers? "I had joint custody, so I limited
my involvement to when my kids were gone," she says. "They never
met anyone—not even as a date standing at the door—unless he
was really important to me."

The irony of Daley's arrangement is that she was probably having
more sex than her married counterparts. "Married couples have the
lowest sexual frequency of their entire lives when they have teenage
children," says certified sex therapist Darcy Luadzers, Ph.D. Partly
that's because raising teenagers entails a high level of conflict. But
privacy plays a part, too; teens stay up later than we do, and they
are attuned to what may be going on behind the bedroom door.

To reclaim their sex lives, Dr. Luadzers counsels *married parents
of teens* to "lock your bedroom door and make random use of your
stereo or TV. If you turn on your stereo only when you're having
sex, your kids will know what's going on whenever they hear Van
Morrison." Consider switching your sex time from the evening—
when most teens are watching movies or surfing the Web—to
Saturday or Sunday mornings, when they're in dreamland.

For *single parents of teens*, a sexual reationship with another person can be painful evidence that a divorce is final. Allow your children to talk out their feelings, then use these chats to broach why
you've opted to get sexually involved. Be clear about your own conditions for sex—both as a way to explain your decision and as a
way to help your children decide if they are ready themselves.

No matter how much your kids squirm and protest, both married
and single parents should talk to their children about sex on a regular
basis. "Allow your teenagers to ask questions," Dr. Luadzers advises.
"But also put boundaries on your privacy." —ELIZABETH LARSEN

This is not a question of age. No matter how young you are, you can't sweep someone off his feet who's lashed in place by apron strings. The real news is that he's not waiting for someone else to come along: He's happy to have you adapt your ways to his mission in life, which is tending to Mummykins.

You've gotten involved with a man who hasn't made you feel good about who you are. Instead he has made you feel uncared for, and you've translated that into feeling "old." You are wise to return his unkindness with independence: Go your own way, and enjoy your travels—and your life—untrammeled.

Oh, and one more thing: In future please date only those men whose wallets hold lots of family photos.

**Q** My mother-in-law has health problems, and she had to move in with us recently. My husband does all he can, but I'm afraid that I'll become her caretaker. She's so manipulative that I didn't mind her living five states away for 27 years. I fear this could kill our marriage.

**A** This could be a reality TV show: How can a marriage survive the manipulative mother-in-law? Let's plan a strategy.

You can help out, but don't burn out. She's your husband's mother, so she's primarily his responsibility. If you haven't told him this before, I wonder if you both often avoid painful topics or if you have trouble saying no. Remember, even the nicest people can be manipulative (and I'm not talking about his mom). There's no harm in setting guidelines. You need to practice saying, "I know this is an enormous job for you. How can I help?"

Have an honest talk with your husband. Agree on how long this arrangement will go on. For instance, it's fair to say that if your mother-in-law becomes bedridden she won't continue to live with you. Divide tasks fairly: You shouldn't be the only one to prepare her meals or take her to the doctor. If you do too much, you could eventually blow up at her—and that will make *you* look like the nut case. Caregiving is exhausting, so use teamwork. This is where your marriage comes in… or caves in.

Couples can care for others, but their commitments to each other come first. A mother-in-law can be a safer target than looking honestly at what may have been a problem before she arrived. The real issue may be in your marriage, where you seem to feel that you don't have any say in this matter.

I hope you'll speak frankly to your husband about what you want personally and in your relationship at this point in life (and not what you think he, or others, expect you to want). Your health, emotional outlook, and 27-year marriage are worth the time investment.

**Q** My wife died almost three years ago, and next spring I am marrying another lady, Mary, who lives about 200 miles away. For the first year I knew Mary, we were just friends. Initially we talked mainly about losing loved ones (she lost a brother five years ago). She has been divorced for five years, with a 16-year-old son, twin girls, and another son in law school. I have three children in their 30s, and though I am retired, Mary will be working for another four years.

I met Mary two years ago, when she oversaw the flower arrangements for the wedding of my oldest daughter. My oldest daughter did not meet her until a few months before the wedding.

When my oldest daughter and her brother learned I had been talking to Mary by phone, they got upset. (My youngest child lives near me and is okay with the situation.) Things got worse when Mary accompanied my sister and another woman on a trip to the Azores last year. When they found out about the trip, my two oldest children called my sister and accused her of "setting me up" with Mary. They even called Mary and made some very vulgar statements, both directly to her and on her voice mail.

My two oldest children feel that Mary is taking advantage of me, and that I am abandoning them. My upcoming marriage to her, they feel, will spoil all our holidays. Neither child wants to set foot in the same house with Mary.

Six months ago, my oldest daughter had my first grand-child. Because she does not want Mary to come near her or her son, I plan on visiting my grandson (300 miles away) by myself. Or I will take Mary, and she will stay at a motel while I visit my grandson.

My oldest daughter still talks to me, but she does not want to discuss Mary at all. My son will not talk to me—even when we were pallbearers at my father-in-law's funeral last spring.

I do not like this situation, but I have no control over my children's behavior. (Mary is not too happy about my two oldest children either.) I still love my children. I have talked to many people; they all tell me I have to live my life.

My plans are to get married, and to celebrate future holidays with Mary. Because my youngest daughter accepts the situation, we will spend some holidays with her and invite her with us on holiday too. How should I handle this situation after I get married?

**A** I won't look for your tribe in the "Family Reunions" section of *Better Homes and Gardens* this year—unless it's a special edition on nuclear family war. That's what your family seems to be waging.

Your children may be suffering from one or more of the Five Family Fables:

1) *Large families are always close.* Nope. Balancing the needs of a large family demands tremendous effort—from every member of that family. Given enough generations and enough needs, people often begin naturally to go their separate ways.

2) *A death in the family brings everyone together.* 'Fraid not! A death in the family is a crisis. It tends to emotionally overextend all family members. The death of a significant family member—a mother, for example—creates a giant hole that survivors will be falling into for years to come.

3) *Coping with death is easier for an affluent family.* Think again. Families frequently fight about money in the months after a death. It beats dealing with their grief.

4) *The term "for your own good" is used only by adults trying to control a child's behavior.* Sorry, no. Adults are equal-opportunity moralizers. If they feel menaced by another family member's behavior—especially if that conduct departs from the norm or threatens to downgrade a status or role—adults (and adult children) will inflict this phrase on anyone: "I'm telling you this only for your own good, Dad...."

5) *Everyone rejoices in happy endings, such as the remarriage*

*of a widow or widower.* Wa-a-a-ay unlikely. A few families
may work this way, but many others will not embrace the
blushing bride or groom. Why? Because they do not want
life to move on. Because they dislike, envy, or resent the
new spouse. Or because selfishness is a universal human
trait and they are loath to share the family's financial assets
with an auslander.

To your credit, you have mapped out a strategy for pro-
ceeding, even if that course of action is predicated (correctly,
in my view) on a great deal of sadness and resignation on
your part. You will miss your two older children and those
holidays you once celebrated together. For many families,
the passage of time heals the hurt caused by a marriage such
as the one you have planned with Mary, allowing everyone
—or at least those willing to give it the old family try—to
experience the closeness and connections they had always
enjoyed. After all, those two sensations are the primary
*raison d'être* for being *en famille*.

In other families, by contrast, bridging a schism like
the one you describe calls for the help of a professional.
Ask your children to meet with you and a family therapist
skilled in conflict resolution. Involving an outsider may
help you get to the bottom of—and dispel—all this unbri-
dled animosity.

Speaking of which, I can't quite divine why your two
oldest feel so alienated by the recent developments in your
domestic scene. Their anger could stem from one of the
Five Family Fables I outlined above, of course, but I would
also urge you to find out if "there's something about Mary";
might there be some aspect of her behavior that has legiti-
mately prompted these reactions? I can only speak to the

half of the story you've presented; I just hope there isn't another half you know nothing about!

What I can say for certain is this: Nothing will be gained by severing ties or escalating the hostilities. Regardless of your older children's feelings for Mary, it was wrong for them to be so cruel to you and her.

Move ahead with your plans, but don't move out of their lives. Maintain as much contact as your children will allow. Enjoy your relationship with Mary and with the family you have, and look forward to savoring the bonds you are sure to forge with her family as well.

**Q** My son hasn't given my grandson "the sex talk" yet even though the kid is 16. He and his wife aren't the most open people in the world, so I don't have faith that they're going to do it. I can see my grandson getting into situations soon where he's going to need to know something, and I think he respects my opinions, so I'm about to step in. How should I deal with this?

**A** You're wading into rough water here. An unsolicited sex-ed initiative shouts that you have no faith in your son as a father—or maybe it was your use of that phrase that shouted it. And by the way, are you actually an expert on sexual matters? What do you really know about sex? (Being a dynamo in bed doesn't count as knowledge.) Proceed with caution, if at all: Bad information can be more harmful to adolescents than no information at all.

To avoid firing a salvo at your son, you might ask him— humbly, respectfully—if you could be helpful in teaching your grandson about sex. When he demurs, as I hope he will, tell him about a Princeton, New Jersey-based organization called HiTOPS (www.Hitops.org), which is dedicated to educating young people about sexual health.

If you're smart, you'll leave it at that. You've registered your concern, and you have also given him a resource he can use. It's his job to follow up.

That said, you've got a valuable role beyond giving him the nuts and bolts of bada-bing. You can teach your grandson a few things about romance and intimacy simply by shooting the breeze with him.

"Kids love to hear their grandparents' stories of their romantic escapades, of love lost, of being dumped and how they survived," says Arthur Kornhaber, M.D., president of The Foundation of Grandparenting and the author of *The Grandparent Guide: The Definitive Guide to Coping with the Challenges of Modern Grandparenting*. This way, when your grandson asks questions, giving him candid, honest answers will be helpful to him—and not disrespectful to your son.

Finally, your worries about his lack of knowledge are probably unnecessary. Public schools start teaching sex education in the fourth or fifth grade nowadays, so I'll bet your grandson knows the basics, whether he's letting on or not. Most kids get in over their heads with sex because they're short on impulse control, not information. Can you teach him that?

Your son and daughter-in-law may not be the world's most forthcoming parents, but do you realize that your grandson is fortunate indeed to have them on the scene? In the United States, more and more grandparents are being asked (or forced) to step in to serve as surrogate parents when their own children abdicate the job. The reasons for this dereliction of parental duty are many—they range from lifestyle "choices" such as alcohol or drug abuse by a parent to neglect or physical or sexual abuse of a child—but the results are frequently the same: Grandparents find themselves becoming new parents just when they were preparing to embark on that richly deserved second childhood.

According to statistics supplied by the United States Census Bureau, 2,426,730 grandparents reported they were "responsible for the basic needs of grandchildren" in the year 2000. That means millions of your contemporaries all across the country have no choice but to hold that awkward "sex talk"—with their grandchildren.

# Afterword

I'VE ALWAYS BRIDLED at the phrase "All good things must come to an end." Whenever someone has the ill fortune to utter it in my presence, I consistently shoot back, "Who designed *that* brilliant system?" Still, I've learned to survive endings by viewing them as kernels of the next great thing.

And so it is with this book. You and I have journeyed a while together. We've discussed finding new love, making love (and making it last), and enduring the messy parts of life. I hope we will continue the voyage a while longer, for this is one vessel that we are clearly in together: We're all still figuring out the verities and perplexities of sex, love, and relationships for grownups. This puzzling-out process is likely to persist long after we've parted.

AARP's 2004 Sexuality Study revealed that the vast majority of respondents deeply value their relationships. Sex, the interviewees felt, may not be wasted on the young, but it's hardly their exclusive playground; sex remains enjoyable well into the later years, and the majority of survey respondents would be unhappy if they could never have it again—an outlook comedically captured by author Patsy Stagner in the subtitle of her book, *Baby Boomer Bachelorette: How to Have Sex at Least Once More Before You Die*.

These ruminations make me think it's no accident that the average age of people who seek therapy at Sexual Health Counseling Services in Ann Arbor, where I practice, is north of 50. The older you get, I believe, the better you grow at framing the eternal questions—even if those queries concern something as seemingly mundane as the endless search for love. You've had a bit more time to come up for air, to look around, to think about yourself and perceive the ways in which your personality has been shaped by the lifetime of experiences you've weathered—some traumatic, others transcendent.

In the preceding pages, I hope you've found some of your own questions answered—even those hazy, yet-to-be articulated ones that have been tugging at the sleeves of your conscience. I hope you've felt that sense of what I call "the long bench of humanity": We all sit down together; we all have problems, and we all get stumped for answers. Think of it as an exercise in communal reassurance. It's gratifying to learn that nobody is perfect, but that almost everybody gets up each morning wanting to give the best of themselves to their relationships.

In many ways, writing about human relationships—how we seek them, how we keep them—evokes memories of summer camp. You share a set of experiences that makes you fast friends with a new group of people. Then, about two-thirds of the way through the enterprise, you realize this glorious adventure is coming to a close.

This is a very sobering point for me—the irreversible shift from being in the thick of it to saying goodbye to all that. It also imparts an indelible sense of writer's regret, for there is still so much I want to explore—about people and their capacity for change, about the shared exploration that is a relationship, about the cultivation of healthy sexuality that has been my lifelong professional quest.

In a perfect world, I would figure out how to cram everything I want to say into one book. Sadly, I cannot. But I console myself with these lines from the famous Maya Angelou poem, which I've pinned to the wall beside my computer:

> *For so long we tried to be perfect in every way*
> *And now when we think about the women we've become,*
> *We realize we're better than perfect;*
> *We are real.*

Despite the number of sobering stories I've heard related in my office, my view of human relations remains rosy, not glum. Hope is the first thing germinated by any realistic appraisal of a problem—and the deeper the problem, I've noticed, the stronger the hope that springs from a glimpse of its solution. This book has tackled how to honestly assess one's predicament—how to appraise a situation and devise some practical strategies for resolving it—all without losing your sense of humor (one of the most effective utensils in humankind's emotional toolbox). So whatever relationship malady may currently afflict your own life, take heart in the knowledge that a powerful antidote to it probably lies within easy reach. Or as Elmer DeWitt once wrote, "If you think you're too small to have an impact, try going to bed with a mosquito."

In *Modern Love*, I've continually built on six themes. These are everyday things that can—over time—have an extraordinary impact on your life. I've attempted to weave these through each answer as appropriate, but let me recap them here:

*Live a life of connections.* Have a wallet full of photos of friends and family. Even if that "perfect" love eludes you, connections to others will give your life meaning.

*Don't be afraid to try something new.* Or, better yet, feel the fear and try it anyway. As T. S. Eliot phrased it in *Four Quartets*, "Love is most nearly itself / When here and now cease to matter / Old men ought to be explorers."

*Expect your relationships to be like your cars.* Despite all the maintenance you devote to them, they are likely to break down from time to time. Sometimes they may even involve you in collisions. (See points 1 and 2 for how to survive these.)

*Abandon either/or thinking.* That Hegelian dialectic is powerless to sort out human connections. Given life's organic complexity, it's better to stay open to plurality, diversity, and the fact that one problem may have 10 different solutions—all of them imperfect.

*Take time to celebrate.* The very ordinariness of life is what is spectacular about living. Ask anyone who's been through a crisis and they'll tell you that what they want most out of life is the restoration of normalcy: Listening to the back door slam as you come home at the end of a long day. Holding a steaming cup of coffee in cold hands. Smelling the earth on the first day of spring. However corny it may sound, everyday normal is the best thing we've got going.

*And finally, love.* This is where words end and life begins. In loving.

In relationships as in sexuality, the normal human impulse is to strive for perfection. Do yourself a favor: Stop trying so hard! Connect to these six ways of approaching life, however, and you may achieve something better than perfect: Beyond the striving and the controlling, beyond orchestrating your life rather than living it, there lies the potential for the real.

—SALLIE FOLEY

DO YOU HAVE A RELATIONSHIP QUESTION that has been "tugging at the sleeves of your conscience," as Sallie Foley puts it? If so, please send it to Modern Love, c/o AARP The Magazine, 601 E Street NW, Washington, D.C. 20049, or to modernlove@aarp.org. You can also visit www.aarpmagazine.org/relationships and submit your question there.

# Resources

## Books

Birch, Robert W. *Sex and the Aging Male: Understanding and Coping with Change.* NY: Pec Pub., 2001.

Blank, Joani, and Anne Whidden. *Good Vibrations: The New Complete Guide to Vibrators.* Down There Press, 2000.

Britton, Patti, and Helen Hodgson. *The Complete Idiot's Guide to Sensual Massage.* NY: Alpha Books/Penguin Group, 2003.

Butler, Robert N., and Myrna I. Lewis. *The New Love and Sex after 60.* NY: Ballantine Books, revised edition, 2002.

Castleman, Michael. *Great Sex: A Man's Guide to the Secret Principles of Total-Body Sex.* NY: Rodale Press, 2004.

Doress, Paula Brown, and Diana L. Siegal. *The New Ourselves, Growing Older: Women Aging with Knowledge and Power.* NY: Simon & Schuster, 1994.

Foley, Sallie, Sally A. Kope, and Dennis P. Sugrue. *Sex Matters for Women: A Complete Guide to Taking Care of Your Sexual Self.* NY: Guilford Press, 2002.

Gottman, John, and Nan Silver. *The Seven Principles for Making Marriage Work.* NY: Three Rivers Press, 2000.

Haines, Staci. *The Survivor's Guide to Sex: How to Have an Empowered Sex Life after Child Sexual Abuse.* San Francisco: Cleis Press, 1999.

Kaufman, Miriam, Cory Silverberg, and Fran Odette. *The Ultimate Guide to Sex and Disability: For All of Us Who Live with Disabilities, Chronic Pain and Illness*. San Francisco: Cleis Press, 2003.

Kroll, Ken, and Erica Levy Klein. *Enabling Romance: A Guide to Love, Sex, and Relationships for People with Disabilities*. Horsham, PA: No Limits Communications, 2001.

Ladas, Alice Kahn, Beverly Whipple, and John D. Perry. *The G Spot and Other Discoveries about Human Sexuality*. New York: Owl Books, 2005.

Laken, Virginia, and Keith Laken. *Making Love Again: Hope for Couples Facing Loss of Sexual Intimacy*. Sandwich, MA: Ant Hill Press, 2002. Discusses re-establishing sexual intimacy after prostate-cancer surgery.

Love, Susan, and Karen Lindsey. *Dr. Susan Love's Menopause and Hormone Book: Making Informed Choices*. NY: Three Rivers Press, 2003.

Metz, Michael, and Barry McCarthy. *Coping with Erectile Dysfunction: How to Regain Confidence and Enjoy Great Sex*. Oakland, CA: New Harbinger, 2004.

McCarthy, Barry, and Emily McCarthy. *Rekindling Desire: A Step-by-Step Program to Help Low-Sex and No-Sex Marriages*. NY: Brunner-Routledge, 2003.

Ogden, Gina. *Women Who Love Sex: An Inquiry into the Expanding Spirit of Women's Erotic Experience*. Cambridge, MA: Womanspirit Press, 1999.

Schwartz, Pepper, and Janet Lever. *The Great Sex Weekend: A 48-Hour Guide to Rekindling Sparks for Bold, Busy, or Bored lovers*. NY: Perigee/Penguin Group, 2000.

Stagner, Patsy. *Baby Boomer Bachelorette: How to Have Sex at Least Once More Before You Die*. JPS Publications, 2004.

Weiner-Davis, Michele. *The Sex-Starved Marriage: A Couple's Guide to Boosting Their Marriage Libido*. NY: Simon & Schuster, 2003.

Zilbergeld, Bernie. *The New Male Sexuality: The Truth about Men, Sex, and Pleasure*. NY: Bantam, 1999.

Zoldbrod, Aline. *Sex Smart: How Your Childhood Shaped Your Sexual Life and What to Do About It*. Oakland, CA: New Harbinger, 1998.

## Websites

### How to find a sex therapist:

American Association of Sex Educators, Counselors, and Therapists (AASECT)
www.aasect.org
(804) 644-3288

### General sex-education questions:

Columbia University Health Education Program
www.goaskalice.columbia.edu

University of Michigan Center for Vulvar Disease
www.med.umich.edu/obgyn/vulva

University of Michigan Sexual Health Counseling Services
www.med.umich.edu/socialwork/shcs

WebMD
www.webmd.com

# Acknowledgments

A WORD ABOUT THE GENESIS of this book: The sex and love column of *AARP The Magazine* has been dishing up relationship advice to older amorists since March of 2003. Recognizing the readership's abiding interest in the topic, editors Ron Geraci and Allan Fallow combed through the hundreds of questions that have been submitted to the magazine over the last two years and culled the most intriguing ones for me to answer in the pages of *Modern Love*. Some of the answers were previously contributed by Hugh O'Neill, my column coauthor; they appear, with his gracious permission, in amended form here.

My thanks to the American Association of Sex Educators, Counselors, and Therapists, especially Director Steve Conley, for ongoing professional leadership and guidance. I am also grateful for the unique environment at the University of Michigan and the many opportunities I have had there. Special thanks to the remarkable leaders of two terrific departments: Kathleen Wade, Director of Social Work, and Timothy Johnson, Chair of the Department of Obstetrics and Gynecology, for their commitment to the entire person's well-being and their unflagging support of Sexual Health Counseling Services.

Speaking of which, I could not have written during these last five months without the constant encouragement of my coworkers at the University: Lisa Engel Evans, Claudia Kraus Piper, Jenn Sanders, and Casey Wilhelm. I am also indebted to a group of colleagues whose psychological insights are woven throughout the book: Martie Martin Conner, Mike Kaplan, Peggy Kleinplatz, Barry McCarthy, Laura Nitzberg, Dale Simmerman, Dennis Sugrue, and Daniela Wittmann.

All three of my children contributed astute observations from the other side of 50; to them, my heartfelt thanks.

Kudos are also due Anne Segall and Steve Foley, who tirelessly listened to rough drafts read aloud and steadily kept me going with their thoughtful perspectives and commentary.

My deepest thanks go to the editors of AARP Books—it's nice to know there's an organization beating the drum for people 50 and over. As leader of the editorial team, Hugh Delehanty conceptualized the book and kept the train on the rails. Design director Carl Lehmann-Haupt came up with the cover design and illustrations approach, then worked closely with illustrator Jeffrey Fisher to perfect the original drawings. Book designer Dorrit Green contributed the playful interior page design and typography selections. And throughout, book editor Allan Fallow applied his indefatigable energy, unfailing good humor, and skill at wrangling words when they threatened to bridle on me.

# About the Author

SALLIE FOLEY, M.S.W., is a couples therapist and AASECT-certified sex therapist. She is affiliated with the University of Michigan's Sexual Health Counseling Services and is on faculty at the Graduate School of Social Work, where she teaches courses in the practice of clinical social work.

A member of the medical advisory board of the Intersex Society of North America, Foley is a regular columnist for *AARP The Magazine* and has written about sexual dysfunction and its treatment in many professional journals. She coauthored the popular *Sex Matters for Women: A Complete Guide to Taking Care of Your Sexual Self.*

Foley and her husband, Steve, a clinical psychologist, have three children and live in Ann Arbor, Michigan.